Online Markets
for Writers

Senior Contributing Writers: Jake Cooney, Karen Morrissey, Janet Page, Mark Palmer

Contributing Writers: Ian Alex, Melinda Anderson, Brad Barnes, Todd Barnes, Shayn Bjornholm, Amy Carle, Dan Carlinsky and the American Society of Journalists and Authors, John Climaco, Matthew B. Collins III, Steve DiPietro, Kathy Djonlich, Emily Drain, Daniel Dratch, Thomas Elia, Peter Fiumara, Brian Lavalle, Mark Lavalle, Marisa Lowenstein, Rocio Martinez, James Meyer, Kate O'Sullivan, Denise M. Petronio, Brent Pickett, Todd Pitock and the National Writers Union, Tony Sacco, Susan Spinale, Sarah Stuckey, Lisa Tancredi, Stephen Tesher, Eric Wells, Jennifer Zembrodt, and Ethan Zohn.

Contributors: One World Internetworking: The E-Commerce Applications Company ([800] 519-1112), especially Susan Hamill and Sean Ross and Staci Paley; Writersmarkets.com and Angela Adair-Hoy; Norman Schreiber of the American Society of Journalists and Authors; Cate T. Corcoran of the National Writers Union.

ANTHONY TEDESCO
and PAUL TEDESCO

Online
Markets
for Writers

■ How to
Make Money
by Selling
Your Writing
on the
Internet

AN OWL BOOK

HENRY HOLT AND COMPANY   ■   NEW YORK

Henry Holt and Company, LLC
Publishers since 1866
115 West 18th Street
New York, New York 10011

Henry Holt® is a registered trademark of
Henry Holt and Company, LLC.

Published in Canada by Fitzhenry & Whiteside Ltd.,
195 Allstate Parkway, Markham, Ontario L3R 4T8.

Parts of *Online Markets for Writers* have appeared in
Writer's Market 1998, 1999, and 2000 editions,
published by Writer's Digest Books.

Library of Congress Cataloging-in-Publication Data
Tedesco, Anthony, 1969–
Online markets for writers: how to make money by selling your
writing on the Internet / Anthony Tedesco, Paul Tedesco.—
1st Owl Books ed.
p.   cm.
Includes index.
ISBN 0-8050-6226-2 (pbk.)
1. Authorship—Marketing.   2. Internet (Computer network)
I. Tedesco, Paul, 1973–   II.   Title.
PN161 .T43   2000
070.5'2'02854678—dc21   99-054938

Henry Holt books are available for special promotions and
premiums. For details contact: Director, Special Markets.

First Edition 2000

Designed by Victoria Hartman

Printed in the United States of America

10 9 8 7 6 5 4 3 2 1

Contents

Acknowledgments

We'd like to thank our parents, Tony and Judy Tedesco, for, you know, life. We'd also like to thank our agents, Richard Curtis and Laura Tucker, as well as our editor, Jen Charat, and our acquiring editor, Elise Proulx.

Anthony's first solo thank-you goes to Janet Page, then to Paul for introducing him to Janet Page, then back to Janet, whose love and support and pesto kept Anthony borderline sane through this book's never-ever-ending saga. P.S. What's up, Jess Page.

We'd also like to thank the following people in no particular order so don't read into it: Jordan and Cody Katter, Michelle Manzanares, Amy Robertson, Kirsten Holm and Don Prues and Writer's Digest Books, Ruth Kaplan, Ellen Ullman, Angela Postels, Jenn Lawson, Marcy Ribera, Clancy Ratliff, Kelly Lacy, Katherine Davis, Tiffany O'Meara, Karen Russell, The Zoom Kids, all of Cape Cod, Christopher James and his new CD which rocks and we don't use "rocks" often or ever so buy his CD, Doug Cooney and the whole Cooney crew, Doug E. Fresh and the whole Getfresh Crew, Carole Maccartee, Mr. Ho, Audrey Wozniak, Dana Cronin, Dana Petronio, Peter Adams, Farai Chideya, Deroy Murdock, Jesse and Will Stamell, Ron Lieber, Kelley Lavin, Jennifer Johnson, Karen Grace, Robin Schatz and Marc Perton and WWWAC Writers Group (http://www.wwwac.org), Steve Outing and Amy Gahran and Content Exchange (http://www.content-exchange.com), Valerie Szymkowicz, Scott Matthews, all the contributing writers that you already read on the contributing-writer page, all the contributing writers who aren't on the contributing-writer page because they provided market information confidentially for the sole reason of helping other writers (thanks), Michelle Stern, Sylvia Alvarado and her/Andreas's slate-blue '63 Ford Galaxie convertible with turquoise interior, Gotham United, Rick Siegel, Debbie Ridpath Ohi (author of *Writer's Online Marketplace*), Moira K. Allen (author of *Writing.com*), Cristina Page and Steve Fishman, Laurie Loporchio, Lexington's Swungdees, The Benson Sisters, Suzanne Serrano, Nicole Lamoureaux, Michelle and John Keenan, Marie Frank, Pete Celi, Fatty and Slim Jimmy, Wordwright Critique Service & SFWA, Terry Boothman, Dan Zevin, Linda Weltner, Ed and Linda Colozzi, Michael Counts and Gale Gates Et Al., Deana Stroud and Envé Salon, Karen Salmansohn, Tracy Wuischpard and Bruce Tovsky, John Mecklenburg and Paul Martinek and Jackie Giron and the LW crew, Jim and Cynthia Tunstall, Gay Young, Victoria Sanders, Bill Dealy, Katherine Cogswell, Amedeo Modigliani, Gamera and all our friends on Monster Island, every member of the Rahaim, Katter, Tedesco, and Rosa families, and every single one of you ravishingly beautiful people whom we're forgetting under this frenetic deadline.

Online Markets
for Writers

Introduction:
Hello/How to Use This Book

ANTHONY TEDESCO

I know, I know. The Internet is basically a big hype sandwich, perennially projected to deliver infinite everything within the nearly foreseeable future, millennium millennium, and a virtual hoorah to boot.

But I hereby do solemnly swear: There's nothing virtual or pending about online writing markets. They're here now and they're real. Featuring real editors with real checks which can really be cashed for money. (Real money.) You just need to know where the lucrative markets are and how to adapt your plenitude of print writing skills to the online publishing world.

That's where we, the co-authors, come in. We're brothers (hi, Mom) and also online writers and editors who've been on both sides of the online-magazine query letter for seven years. Seven years. That's roughly 1,400 years in online-writing time. We're rickety, and wise, or at least wise enough to enlist the help of two of the largest and most pervasive and pioneering writer organizations, the National Writers Union (NWU) and the American Society of Journalists and Authors, as well as 25 of the industry's top online editors and writers, and the most physically attractive gaggle—yeah, I said it—gaggle of contributing writers ever assembled into one physically attractive assembly.

Here's what it means to you:

We've got the first-ever database of pay-and-policy information for more than 200 paying online markets—listed alphabetically and indexed by subject—including information confidentially provided by the market's freelance writers; we've got a sample boilerplate contract so you know what's out there; we've got the NWU's standard Webzine contract so you know what should be out there; we've got an online editor's favorite electronic query and why it's her favorite; we've got personality, walking personality, talking personality; we've got tips on absolutely positively hopefully everything, from negotiating electronic rights and rates to a glossary with the only cyber terms you actually need to know and a crash-course for the only HTML you actually need to know; and we've got Web resources for writers recommended by the expert online writers and editors who are using them.

One last thing, a very important last thing that should've been the first thing in neon capital blinking letters: *We'll update this book for you for free.* Mosey over to http://www.marketsforwriters.com, sign up for our free update e-mail newsletter (or some name that's a little more catchy), and we'll e-mail you any changes in the text.

That's where you come in. In case the market doesn't notify us of the change, please let us know yourself (anthony@marketsforwriters .com). We'll credit you for the update and you'll be the most popular kid in town. Also, send us your (confidential) experiences writing for the markets listed so we can spread the word in our free newsletter and future editions. Also #2: send us any markets that we've missed, send us any feedback on our book, send us any preferences for future editions. We like getting things. (Thanks.)

Welcome to the Internet

Section 1

HISTORY OF THE INTERNET
IN 10 WORDS OR LESS

PAUL TEDESCO

So here's the story in brief: You got the government in the late '60s and you got a few computers scattered around the country that are big enough to stop a bus. The threat of nuclear war is looming large and the question of communication under such a siege is imminent. As online writer and civilian, you don't need to know why. All you need to know is that those government people connected a bunch of these machines, mostly at universities around the country, and created a "network." This network was the beginning of the Internet. It allowed them to "talk" to each other and share government-people-type information and transfer data back and forth. Just them. Back and forth. You still don't need to know why.

Time goes on, more computers are added from universities, the network grows.

Suddenly it's the early '90s. The network hits pop culture and people all over the world are e-mailing each other without checking spelling. The World Wide Web portion of the Internet is introduced to the masses, thus allowing pictures and images to be viewed through an application called a "browser." One of the main functions of the Web is the "linking" of information from one Web site to another—regardless of where the physical Web site pages live geographically. Everyone starts making graphical pages (Web sites). Linking runs amuck. Life is good.

Section 2

EVEN BRIEFER HISTORY OF
ONLINE WRITING AND PUBLISHING

PAUL TEDESCO

Picture this: It's September 1993 and the first Web browser, Mosaic, is introduced. Peter Adams, Thomas Elia, and I begin publishing the Trincoll Journal weekly online. We took what began as a HyperCard stack publication (which is like a bunch of notecards stapled together) based out of Pete's dorm room at Trinity College and switched it over to the Web and to the world.

At that time, Web publishing consisted of two publications: our Trincoll Journal, published weekly, and *Wired* magazine's HotWired, published sporadically. That was it. Web pages were rudimentary and coded the old-fashioned way—by hand and in SimpleText. The pages themselves were limited to a medium-gray background, a royal blue link color, and left alignment. After a couple months and new beta versions, we could center-align pictures. It was like payday.

Web publishers can now incorporate audio, video, and animation. These types of multimedia capabilities separate Web publishing from traditional publishing.

Another major difference is revenue. Yes, ads are being sold—nearly $2 billion worth of ads in 1998, according to studies cited at CyberAtlas (http://www.cyberatlas.com). But those same studies are showing that a whopping 71 percent of that advertising revenue is going only to the 10 leading publishers. The rest of the online publishing world is struggling for a stake, and searching for other revenue streams.

(A side note: While online magazines struggle and search, they should also be sending you money for your freelance services. You provide a service and require compensation, like their compensated accountants, lawyers, computer supplier, long-distance phone carrier, and Con Edison. Do you think they tell Con Edison it won't get paid until online-publishing ventures are profitable?)

All right, back to advertising. The cavalry is already en route. One report also cited at CyberAtlas found that "the annual growth rate of Internet advertising far surpasses any other media. With a rate of 111.8 percent, the next best percentage of growth is cable television at 13 percent."

Online publishing is here to stay. Investors are pouring money into the industry, and Wall Street is still going public with publishers who haven't shown anything that resembles a hint of a profit, making paper millionaires out of everyone. The good news is that some online writing markets actually provide stock options to freelance writers. Good news #2: investor boons are continuing to bolster online freelance-writing budgets. Online market rates have already risen to that of print publications; opportunities abound for $2/word gigs and steady work reaping thousands per month.

More good news? It's easy to start your online journalism forays.

Get a computer. If your computer doesn't come with a built-in modem, buy a modem that you can afford, and know that the number represented on the box (e.g., 28.8, 56.6, etc.) is how fast you'll be connected. So pick your poison because the price is directly related to the connection speed, and connection speed is directly related to sanity . . . or lack thereof.

Then find an internet service provider (ISP) in your local area. (See http://www.thelist.com for an exhaustive list of ISPs.) (Yes, we know you don't have access yet, but this list is worth a little legwork—try a connected friend or a cyber cafe, or go to your local library, since most are equipped with computers that provide access to the Internet.) These ISPs are people that put you "online." They're much like the Keebler Elves except, instead of putting Fudge Stripes in the oven, they answer your modem and connect its call to the Internet. And to be fair, they're probably a bit taller.

So your only costs are computer, modem, and usually some fixed monthly rate for the ISP people to keep baking snacks and making sure you get online when you want. The Internet itself is free. Discussion groups, chat rooms, Web surfing, search engines, research resources—and e-mail for sending pitches and clips to online-writing markets.

Section 3

A COMPLETE GLOSSARY OF THE ONLY
CYBER TERMS YOU ACTUALLY NEED TO KNOW

ANTHONY TEDESCO

There are about 7 million techie terms currently asphyxiating the online world. I'm pretty sure the people at *Wired* magazine made up most of them—for fun. After amassing your first billion dollars, you may want to dedicate your waking time to learning all of those terms, for fun. Until then, let's stick to the basics—just a handful of the only know-how you need to successfully pitch an online editor and deliver your completed piece. Tech-savvy writers forgive us/forge ahead to other chapters, as we cheerfully begin with . . .

- *Attachment:* This refers to a file attached to an e-mail message (e.g., a file formatted in Microsoft Word, a digital photograph, a video clip, etc.). Somewhere in your e-mail application is the option to "Attach" a file. Don't do it. Well, don't do it unless you get permission from the editor and coordinate the process. It's always safer to just save your file as "text only" and then copy and paste it into the body of your e-mail message. (See "Sending Your Query" and the sample query on pages 22–24.)
- *Browser:* Software that lets you view all that is on the Web (Netscape Communicator and Microsoft Internet Explorer are the two biggies).
- *Domain Name:* This is essentially the first four "words" in a URL, only without the "http://www." part (e.g., "http://www.marketsfor writers.com/index.html" is a URL, "marketsforwriters.com" is the

domain, or the root). Usage: Editor says, "At the end of your column, list all of the URLs within the marketsforwriters.com domain that describe writing markets." You say, "No." But you understand what the editor meant by "domain."

- *E-Zine:* Short for electronic magazine. Perhaps a little more funky and independent than mainstream corporate online publications. Perhaps not.

- *Flash, Shockwave, VRML, Java, JavaScript:* These applications are exciting developments, enhancing Web sites with special effects such as animation and three-dimensionality, if that's a word. Truth be told, though, very few Web sites incorporate these effects, especially not sites that are interested in paying for professional writing, and especially not in ways you need to know as a professional writer. The effects still tend to crash systems. You really don't have to know them. (If you *just gotta* know their specifics, http://www.netscape.com covers most of them.)

- *HTML:* As an online writer, you don't need to know what it stands for (HyperText Markup Language) and you don't need to know how to write HTML code (though we provide a crash course on pages 10–11 to put you in an editor's "celestial" category). Know that HTML is the universal code your browser reads and translates into living, breathing Web pages. HTML tags look like this: "<B>This part would be in bold text<B>" thanks to Mr. HTML. If you're interested in the full code gamut, most browsers have a "View Source" feature which lets you, yes, view the source code (HTML tags and other code goodies) of any Web page.

- *Link:* A word or phrase or picture or anything on a Web site that you can click on, sending you to whatever URL that thing is linked to. Text links often appear in a different color from the rest of the text.

- *Listserv (no "e" at the end):* Software that lets people sign up for or sign off of mailing lists.

- *Mailing List:* An ongoing, e-mail discussion group. People in the group e-mail their opinion/whatever to one address and the message is forwarded to everyone in group. Mailing lists are a good resource for acquiring answers about particular topics (there's a mailing list for even the most obscure topics). They also serve as a way to unite these topical interests into a community of people who share them.

- *Search Engine:* Also called a "portal" because everyone wants to be your starting point into the Internet world, and all "portals" are currently endearing to Wall Street. Go to the site of a search engine, type in what you're searching for on the Web, and it gives you URLs of pages that have that information. Of course, they give about 5 million URLs, but you can keep narrowing your search down until the findings are specifically what you want found.

- *URL:* You don't need to know what it stands for. Just know it's the "Internet address" or location of any page on the Internet (again, e.g., "http://www.strongbat.com"). Editors will often ask you to include related URLs with a story, so they can include related links for readers.

Section 4

A COMPLETE CRASH COURSE ON THE ONLY
HTML YOU ACTUALLY NEED TO KNOW

ANTHONY TEDESCO

A few online editors will request (and the rest will emphatically appreciate) your including basic HTML tags in your text. They never want you to design the whole story—just to apply basic formatting. Most e-mail applications give you the option of automatically translating the body of your text message into HTML. In that case, use it. If your e-mail application doesn't provide that option, get one that does. If, like me, you're too broke and/or lazy to upgrade your e-mail application, here's all the HTML you need to know. *Before* saving your article as "text only," insert these tags where it's appropriate:

To bold text:	\<B>the bold words\</B>
To italicize text:	\<I>the italic words\</I>
For a line break:	\ where you want the break
To set a new paragraph:	\<P> at the end of a paragraph starts you on the next paragraph by adding the equivalent of two line breaks—one break, then one return line before the next sentence.

| To create a text link | <A HREF="http://www.marketsforwriters.com"> this is the text that will be linked, sending people who click on it to http://www.marketsforwriters.com—don't forget those quotation marks.</A> |

That's it. Really. The site will handle the forms and graphics and jargon. You're a hero/heroine for handling the above tags, making your text-only article more accurate to the text you want stylized (without the tags in your text-only article, the editor wouldn't know what was supposed to be bold, italic, the end of a paragraph, or a link to another site or page for more information), and making it easier to read for the editor and easier to format for the designer.

Writing for Online Markets

ANTHONY TEDESCO

INTRODUCTION

There's one thing we should get straight. If you're looking to learn all those geek-speak emoticon hieroglyphic winkey-smiley code symbols, you've come to the wrong book. This is not about cyber-centric parlance. There will be no twelve-letter acronyms in lieu of conversational phrases. There will be no obscure technical references ending with three exclamation points denoting excitement about said obscure technical references.

Sure, there are some Net users who communicate almost exclusively in this cryptic high-tech vernacular. But they're a minority. An astute little space-alien minority.

Most online editors and writers aren't techies writing for techies about techie things. We're just opportunists who've tapped a new market—151 million online readers strong, according to *Computer Industry Almanac,* and growing faster than any other mass medium. For us, technology is a means, not an end. We've supplemented our newsstand options with the Net, but we're still writing and selling the same cultural/comical/whatever-ical pieces we've been writing for traditional media.

Not *exactly* the same. The same topics, yes. But writing for the Internet and the Internet's audience does have its distinct nuances, and knowing these nuances will help you sell articles online. Here are some tips, traps, and tricks (trying saying that ten times fast) that Paul and I have learned from being on both sides of the online magazine query letter for the last seven years. And although we're fairly certain that we know absolutely everything, we've also complemented our omni-science/egomania/this section with insightful interviews from many of the industry's top online editors and writers. You know, just in case.

Section 1

KNOW YOUR READERS

Now that I've established that all Net users aren't necessarily quintessential tech geeks, let's dispel a few more mistaken tacks. Here's a quick look at the official landscape of online readers, care of the research firms gathered at CyberAtlas (http://www.cyberatlas.com):

- the average age of Internet users is 32 years old;
- 64 percent of all Internet users have at least a college degree (Nielsen Media Research);
- 46 percent of Internet users in North America are female (Nielsen/Commerce Net)
- Internet users have a median household income of $59,000 (Graphic, Visualization, and Usability Center).

There. A few basic stats to hopefully quell that research temptation. Now forget them, because 151 million online readers means online readers are really whoever you want them to be. Although the medium still yearns for conclusive tools for mapping its users, writers have to stop thinking of "Internet Users" as one big Internet-using group. Writers don't have to know what interests "Internet Users," just what interests the Internet users who are reading their targeted online market.

Actually, the writer's job is usually even one more step removed than that. You don't have to know what interests the Internet users who are reading a particular online market, just what the editor thinks are the interests of those Internet users.

So spare yourself the general Internet surveys, demographic reports, and latest hyped-up breakthrough press releases. Your best bet is to simply read/absorb the target publication because it represents the editor's latest guesswork at what interests his or her readers.

After this mandatory perusal, you can even ask editors for more reader-profile information in your query. Online editors recognize how difficult it is to conclusively know readerships, and many appreciate the extra effort. Some online writers interviewed for this book recommended requesting more information from editors not only because it helps in tailoring queries but also for its advantages in establishing a willing, working rapport.

Section 2

FIND YOUR TARGET MAGAZINES

With so many different people online—people of all ages, all academic backgrounds, all incomes, all cultures—you can easily find readers interested in topics that interest you, as well as online magazines catering to those interests. The trick, of course, is finding online magazines catering to your interests that also pay writers for content. There are more than 200 paying online markets for you in this book, but all it takes is a little foraging to customize your own list of potential online publications.

A good place to start is on the pages of the very same markets you've targeted in traditional media. Most print publications have companion online magazines that quite often feature original online writing. Check the masthead page for their corresponding URL (Internet address), or peruse the advertising pages for Web site promotions. Even publishing companies with the resources of many magazines usually opt for creating original online brands merely rooted in their print counterparts. Condé Nast, for example, publishes the "online versions" of its magazines *Gourmet* and *Bon Appétit* under the online brand *Epicurious Food* (http://www.food.epicurious.com), with 80 percent original online content, though not all of that is open to freelancers.

You can occasionally find a print publication's online version by simply typing the publication's title into your Web browser (http://

www.thetitle.com). If that fails, try entering the title into one of the Web's many search engines.

Here are a few examples of pervasive print publications with sister online ventures:

- *Boston Globe* online (http://www.boston.com)
- *USA Today* online (http://www.usatoday.com)
- *New York Times Interactive* (http://www.nytimes.com)
- *Internet World* online (http://www.iworld.com)
- *Advertising Age* online (http://www.adage.com)
- *The Village Voice* online (http://www.villagevoice.com)
- *GQ, Mademoiselle, Glamour,* and *Details* online (http://www.swoon .com)
- *Playboy* online (http://www.playboy.com)
- *Gourmet* and *Bon Appétit* online (http://www.food.epicurious.com)
- *Wired* online (http://www.hotwired.com)
- *The Wall Street Journal Interactive Edition* (http://www.wsj.com)

Another way to locate online magazines with your target readers are directories and electronic newsstands, though there are so many online magazines on the Internet that it's easy to get overwhelmed with options and often difficult to discern whether or not they pay their freelancers without actually querying the editor. The good news: If you can muster the perseverance, the Internet is your best shot at securing a patron publication for your most idiosyncratic of interests. Here are some resources:

- John Labovitz's E-Zine List (http://www.meer.net/~johnl/ e-zine-list/index.html) touts almost 2,000 online magazines, searchable by title, subject, and even keywords.
- F5 Ezine Archive (http://www.well.com/conf/f5/ezines.html) features links to other online magazine archives.
- Etext Archives (http://www.etext.org) is home to electronic texts of all kinds.
- Ezine Newsgroup (alt.ezines) is a good place to query the ezine community about any genre of magazine.
- The Well's Publications Area (gopher://gopher.well.com/11/

Publications) offers information on the full gamut of online magazines.

Section 3

ADAPTING YOUR WRITING TO THE WEB

Once you're armed/dangerous with your target list of online markets, you should adapt your writing muse to the nuances of the World Wide Web.

Local Writing for a Global Audience

The words "World" and "Wide" make this first tip so obvious that writers often overlook it. Readers on the Internet hail from all over the world. English is still the standard, but English doesn't mean U.S.-centric. It's just as easy for someone in Seattle to read a particular online magazine as it is for someone from Sri Lanka. Your articles should reflect that diversity—without watering down the distinctions that make it real. Think local details with global appeal.

Take, for example, one of our columns at Crisp (http://www .crispzine.com) entitled "Actor's Journal: Amy Carle rants and rambles about trying to balance her office day job with her theater-group dream job." Amy's writing is so engaging because (a) she's an engaging writer/person, and (b) she infuses her journal entries with personal details such as her coworker's compulsion with keeping the workplace temperature a brisk sub-zero, or the high, clunky, and undoubtedly dangerous heels that she's agreed to dance in for the full run of Chicago-based Roadwork's rendition of *Orestes*.

Is Mr. Sri Lanka going to make it to the show to see the heels? Probably not (his loss). Is it cold in your workplace? I don't know, I don't work with you. But Amy balances these animated details with the bigger picture that people all around the world can relate to: making sacrifices in the pursuit of your passions; dealing with quirky (freaky) coworkers at a job that means little more to you than money for bills while pursuing those passions.

Use Your Own Voice

Along the same lines of personal details, Net readers have a penchant for wanting to know people, real people, real regular Joe/Jody individuals, you. I think it stems from the fact that regular Joe/Jody has always had equal billing to corporate behemoths on the Internet. Basic home pages are as accessible as highfalutin sites, and Net users still prize themselves as anti-establishment, give or take an establishment.

Also, although the Internet is a global gathering, it's a gathering that empowers and connects individuals. This subtle dichotomy was best demonstrated in a *Details* article I read about a Net-spawned amateur exhibitionist who was adamant about her being shy, despite her nude pictures posted on her site. She explained that the only reason she was able to, um, exhibit herself in front of so many people was that she wasn't doing it in front of all those people at once. Each person experienced her "art" individually, at his or her own computer.

Okay, that was a dangerous example, but it's worth illustrating this most pivotal aspect of interactive writing: Although it feels like you're writing for a mass audience called Net users, you're actually communicating with people on a one-to-one basis.

So stay away from third person, which says "distanced," "corporate," "disinterested." Or the collective "We" addressing the collective "You." Opt instead for first person, and don't shy away from your opinions (not that you have to bash them with your cyber-soapbox either; impassioned doesn't have to mean belligerent).

Write in your own voice, not standard written English. Let your vernacular and personality show through, even if you're pitching a service-oriented piece such as a book review or an interview. I want to know less about the book and more about how the book made you feel. (Different markets require different nuances, so confirm this voice with your particular editor—but generally it's the case.)

Were you reading the book at your desk or in a hammock sipping makeshift coladas? Why did you choose the book? Were you feeling down about your best friend, Frank Botts, who gave your Yankees seat to some girl-of-the-week he's trying to impress, as if she'll stick around after watching him inhale eight hot dogs? Were you extra-nervous interviewing Paul Newman not only because of his epic celebrity status but because you spent much of your younger days gazing into his dreamy blue eyes on the *Cool Hand Luke* poster? Do you still have the poster safely stashed away in your room?

Again, study the nuances of your particular market but, far more so than with print readers, Net readers want—even expect—to connect with you as well as your story. Let your article be a window into you as a person and not as a press release.

Brevity and Pace

Fast-paced and brief writing is more effective because Net users have so many other options online and it's just so easy to click away—you have to hook them and hook them fast, complementing the visually oriented medium with soundbite-esque copy. Furthermore, computer screens are more difficult to read than traditional paper pages. The screen is usually small and the area for your text is even smaller. Net users don't want to scroll and scroll to finish a piece—they even go so far as to liken excessive scrolling to a drowning feeling, having to go deeper and deeper into a Web page. (You wouldn't want to drown cute little Net users, now would you?)

Brevity is also important to keep download times low (the time readers have to sit around waiting for a page to load onto their screens). Text is data, and while not as cumbersome as images, video, or sound, long text files can cause similar delays.

Incorporating Technology

I'll turn the rest of this section over to Paul "More-Tech-Savvy-Than-Anthony" Tedesco.

(Hi.) When writing for such a technologically cutting-edge medium as the Internet, there are two things to consider: (a) it's not print; and (b) it's not print. Once you understand that, the next step is: (c) it's not print. Kidding (not very well). No, fine, extremely patient readers, (c) is actually understanding what this medium has that print doesn't offer, and incorporating those technologies into your creative process and editor pitches.

Note: You don't have to know the mechanisms that make the technologies work. (We online editors would love it if you did, but then we'd love you to do the rest of our jobs too so we could just lounge poolside.) All you have to know is what's out there—what available technology *could* be used to enhance your article. (And how much fatter your freelance check should be for coming up with such a tech-savvy sidebar.)

Here are a few technologies that could enhance your article:

Audio and Video

Yes, you can incorporate high-quality audio and video right into online articles. Although the download times and streaming advantages are cutting the waiting time for readers, your best bet is to limit yourself to short clips. An article about dining on the Italian Riviera could include not only key phrases for ordering, but actual audio clips of the phrases so readers can hear how they are pronounced. At Crisp, instead of merely including photos of clothing from the innovative, up-and-coming designers of Space Girl, we added short video clips from their fashion show so readers could see how the clothes move on the body.

Links

Links are words or images that can be clicked on to send Net users to another page or site. Almost every company and institution is on the Web now, so if you refer to one, you can link its name to its site.

This concept also goes for references and official home pages of celebrities. If you're writing about it, chances are that there is another relevant article or image out on the Web somewhere that can be linked to, so just as you would do conventional research for any article, search the Web for sites or pages that are relevant to your own piece. The Web is an extremely large database that can be accessed and utilized by the click of a button for the good of humankind, or at least for your freelance check.

For example: an interview with Pamela Anderson could include a sidebar of links to all 14 billion of her fan sites. An article on ginger-root could include links to recipes with ginger available at the many food sites on the Internet.

Chats and Bulletin Boards

Chats and bulletin boards are two of the most widely used aspects of the Web because, at the root of it all, the Web is chock full of people who like to talk and share and complain with other people. If you interview someone, consider asking them to participate in a live chat with readers/fans for a half hour or field questions over a short period on a bulletin board (to plug their latest starry project, of course). Or even just make yourself available to readers with follow-up questions. That sort of access and personal connection means a lot to online readers—which means a lot to online editors.

Java

Java is still so quirky that many sites don't include it. Readers don't like to have their computers crash. Keep an eye out as its usage becomes more stable. An example of incorporating Java into a story is doing a piece on stocks featuring a real-time stock ticker.

Cybercasts

You can not only review a concert or band, you can broadcast it live over the Internet with your article. Check out SonicNet (http://www .sonicnet.com) for inspiration.

Section 4

QUERYING ONLINE EDITORS

Okay, you've found the online magazine that makes your heart go "pitter-patter," and you've honed the piece you consider your Pulitzer Prize–winner. Now what?

At the risk of sounding redundant: Remember to read through the online magazine that made your heart go "pitter-patter" before sending your article. Online editors are just like print editors, only a little cooler (kidding): We don't want a 12,000-word fiction book excerpt if all we publish is breaking news.

Query an editor first with a short e-mail (see sample, page 22). Electronic querying definitely has its advantages: You don't have to pay postage and you don't have to wait for delivery. It still may take a few days for an editor to respond, but the entire process usually takes much less time than with print queries.

Obviously it's best to send your e-mail directly to the appropriate editor. Sometimes, however, his or her e-mail isn't listed on the masthead of the magazine. Fret not. You still have a few options.

Option one: You can rummage through the site until you find a general editorial e-mail address (e.g., "editorial@thetitle.com" or "feedback @thetitle.com") or even the ubiquitous e-mail address of the site's Webmaster (technical overseer) who will probably do you the favor of forwarding your query—unless he or she is particularly busy doing [insert obscure technical task] or he or she just doesn't feel like it. Let's face it, with a title like Webmaster and the perceived power to crash your computer and then charge a celebratory bottle of Dom to your credit card, he or she can do whatever he or she wants, whenever he or she wants to.

Option two shows a little resourcefulness of your own, though don't tell anyone I showed you. Even though an editor's e-mail address might not be listed on the magazine's masthead, it doesn't mean it doesn't exist, and it doesn't mean you can't find it. Sites such as WhoWhere? (http://www.whowhere.com) and Four11 (http://www. four11.com) have gathered millions of e-mail addresses from the Internet so you can get in touch with your long-lost best high-school pal or fave celebrity. As well as, of course, the editor who's going to jump for joy after reading your revolutionary query.

Yes, the non-joy-jumping editor in me says you shouldn't send me e-mails directly, I'm busy, you shouldn't risk simultaneous submissions, and you shouldn't pitch to me over the phone. But then I'm also a freelance writer doing all of those things for the advantages they provide.

Make your own decision. And mum's the word.

(Mum's not the word for the following e-mail query letter sample and insights provided by editor Eileen Gunn.)

Section 5

SAMPLE ELECTRONIC QUERY LETTER WITH ·
TIPS FROM ONLINE EDITOR EILEEN GUNN

Eileen Gunn, managing editor of GORP—Great Outdoor Recreation Pages (http://www.gorp.com) was generous enough to share her favorite query, which was sent to her from writer Todd Whitesel.

From: Todd Whitesel <ohioice@mailhost.day.ameritech.net>
To: eileeng@gorp.com
Subject: Query-Whiteshell Provincial Park, Manitoba

Where the boreal forest overlaps the Canadian Shield is known to ecologists as the boreal shield. As the largest of Canada's fifteen terrestrial ecozones, it is clear that the boreal shield plays a vital role in the north. To explore this land of lakes, bogs, jack pines, and granite, a trip to Manitoba's Whiteshell Provincial Park provides visitors with numerous ways to learn about the shield country.

At 672,334 acres, Whiteshell is an expansive wilderness that is not widely known outside of Canada. With this in mind I would like to propose an article with the tentative title "Exploring the Shield Country in Manitoba's Whiteshell Provincial Park." This would be an overview type of article and would detail activities such as hiking, canoeing, and fishing, as well as unique features including Aboriginal petroforms, a meteorite lake, and a pond with surrounding cliffs of 3.75-billion-year-old rock.

Length would be 3,000–4,000 words and could include photos of landscape, lakes, petroforms, etc. I have several photos available for use.

I look forward to your reply and thank you for your consideration.

Sincerely,

Todd Whitesel
ohioice@ameritech.net

Why is it a good query? Eileen explains:

> It's short (180 words). It's very specific, telling me exactly what he wants to write about and why my readers would want to read it. He's got photos. He gives an estimated length. And he communicates all this without trying to hype it—he just lets the idea speak for itself. Also, it contains no attachments or styled text, which gum up my computer.
>
> Todd followed up the query, at my request, with a detailed outline, a very thorough first draft, and then did a few minor additions to the text. The article is up on our site at http://www.gorp.com/gorp/location/Canada/Manitoba/whitesh.htm.

Section 6

INTERNET STYLE

Despite lofty intentions toward a universal Net style, each publication usually exercises its right to reek of quirkiness/branding, a lot more so than in print media. The bottom line is that it's tough to look bad grammatically. The onus is usually on the editor because other than print's *AP Style Manual*, there's no real rulebook governing Net publishing. (Yet.)

Of course, if someone could pull it off, I'd put my little e-dollars on those gifted techno geek guru digerati at *Wired* magazine, revered keepers of all cryptic Netspeak, purveyors of digi-panache, and (you get the picture but I'm still going) undisputed virtual-weight champs of neo-neologisms. Although your editor-to-hopefully-be should be the one purchasing *Wired*'s book as a style manual, you could definitely score some tech-savvy points with him or her by perusing your own copy (especially if you're targeting online publications focused on technology). Their book is called *Wired Style: Principles of English Usage in the Digital Age* (HardWired, 1997), and it's edited by Constance Hale, with the editors of *Wired*.

Section 7

SENDING YOUR QUERY

When you do finally send the article, plee-ease don't send those 12,000 words as an e-mail attachment unless it's been requested. You could be that one writer with one jumbled photo attachment that crashes the editor's computer and all the files that hadn't been backed up, aka, all the files. It could take three days, lots of cash, and numerous sacrifices to the hard-drive deities to get things working again.

Even big attachments that don't crash my system still take years-or-so to come across my humble Internet connection, which means, for years-or-so, I have to watch that little "percentage completed" line inch and inch (and inch) its way to completion in the middle of my morning e-mails. I'd prefer you to save the article in "text only" format, copy the text, and paste it into your e-mail message. Or at least get permission to send it as an attachment. But your best bet with editors is to send your query without clips. Instead, offer to send clips and ask for his or her—greatly varying and often vehement—preferred method of receiving clips (as attachments, as e-mail text, or as URLs pointing to clips on the Web). If you don't have online clips yet, you can offer to mail or fax hard-copy clips.

If the editor does choose to have online clips sent as e-mail text, remember to copy and paste only the text of the article into your e-mail message and double-check the format. Many writers forget, sending formatted articles (with bolds, italics, indents, accents, smart/ hooked quotation marks, etc.) via e-mail that is text only. The result is that the aforementioned article arrives spotted with awry symbols— not awry enough to make the e-mail illegible, just enough to make you (me) crazy trying to read it. See our HTML crash course on page 10 to learn text-only formatting, and send all e-mails to yourself first to make sure they're formatted how you want them.

Section 8

SAMPLE ONLINE-WRITING CONTRACT

TO SHOW YOU WHAT'S OUT THERE

Remember to see sections 11 and 12 for tips on negotiating through these boilerplate contracts.

Sample Contract

Author: _____ SS #: _____

Address: _____

Phone: _____

Purchase Fee: _____ Kill Fee: _____

1. Agreement: a. This letter serves as the independent contractor Agreement between the Author (as above) and Market (herein after referred to as "the Market") regarding the Work, as described below, which the Author will supply to Market for use on Market's site on the World Wide Web of the Internet, not excluding other uses that the Market will determine but always consistent with and subject to the provisions set forth in this Agreement.

2. Work: a. The Author agrees to supply to the Market the Work described in "the Schedule" found below by the date established in the Schedule. The Author will be paid the amount established above for the Work. However, if the Market does not accept the Work, the Market will pay the Author the Kill Fee established above. b. The Author agrees that the Market does reserve the right to revise, edit, condense, adapt, and fact-check; and the Author agrees to cooperate fully at all stages.

3. Ownership: a. The Author acknowledges that the Work will belong solely to and be the exclusive property of the Market in the manner set forth by United States copyright laws. b. For the full term of the copyright and throughout the World, the Author grants to the Market the right to publish the Work and for sixty (60) days following publication the Author will not allow the Work to be reprinted or reproduced, published or in any way displayed in whole or in part until the exclusivity period of sixty (60) days expires. c. The Author will deliver upon the Market's request any and all documents within reasonable requirement of the Market to prove the Market's exclusive rights as stated above and the Author will cooperate in obtaining or protecting copyright as set forth above.

4. Warranties and Indemnities: a. The Author maintains and warrants that the Work will be completely original material, not previously published, and will not violate any copyrights already held by a third party. b. The Author hereby indemnifies and agrees to defend the Market from any claims, suits, action, losses, or damages, including reasonable attorney's fees and disbursements incurred or sustained as a result of the Work.

5. Independent contractor: The Author agrees to be an independent contractor, hired by the Market, and that nothing set forth in the Agreement renders the Author an employee of the Market. The Author is not entitled to the same rights and privileges that the Market provides for employees. Author agrees that responsibility for payment of income and employment taxes does not rest with the Market and as such, the Market will not withhold any monies for this purpose.

6. Confidentiality: The terms and provisions for the Work set forth in this Agreement are confidential and the Author agrees not to make public to a third party anything established herein.

7. Credits: The Market reserves the right to use the Author's byline, biography, and photograph in association with the Work and in advertising, promotion, and marketing the Work and the Market.

8. Expenses: The Author will be wholly responsible for any incurred business expenses throughout the duration of creating the Work and for the term of the copyright.

9. Miscellaneous: Any modifications to this Agreement, when fully executed, must be consented to by both parties in writing. This Agreement can only be interpreted and ruled in accordance with the laws set forth by the State of New York.

Schedule: _____

Description of Work: _____

Date Due: _____

Manner of delivery: _____

Section 9

NWU'S STANDARD WEBZINE CONTRACT TO SHOW YOU
WHAT SHOULD BE OUT THERE

Contract between (Writer) _____
and (Publisher) _____

1. The Writer agrees to prepare an article of _____ words on the subject of:

_____

_____

for delivery on or before _____ (date). The Writer also agrees to provide one revision of the Article.

2. The Publisher agrees to pay the Writer a fee of $_____ within thirty (30)
days of initial receipt of the Article as assigned above. (In other words, an
original and coherent manuscript of approximately the above word count on
the subject assigned, and for which appropriate research was completed.)

3. The Publisher agrees that the above fee licenses one-time World Wide Web
rights only. This use is time-limited to the webzine's publishing cycle. (A new
publishing cycle commences when the home page is completely refreshed.)
All other rights, including but not limited to hard copy, CD-ROM, data base,
archive, proprietary services and other electronic rights are fully reserved by
the Writer and must be negotiated separately.

4. The Publisher agrees to reimburse the Writer for all previously agreed-
upon and documented expenses within fifteen (15) days of submission of
receipts.

5. The Publisher agrees to make every reasonable effort to make available to
the Writer, the final, edited version of the Article while there is still time to
make changes. In the event of a disagreement over the final form of the

Article, the Writer reserves the right to withdraw his/her name from the Article without prejudicing the agreed-upon fee.

6. The Writer guarantees that the Article will not contain material that is consciously libelous or defamatory. In return, the Publisher agrees to provide and pay for counsel to defend the Writer in any litigation arising as a result of the Article.

7. In the event of a dispute between the Writer and the Publisher that cannot be resolved through the National Writers Union (NWU) grievance process, the Writer will have the option of seeking to resolve the matter by arbitration, or in court. If arbitration is chosen, the Writer may be represented by the NWU in any procedures before the arbitrator. The arbitrator's fees shall be shared fifty percent (50%) by the Publisher and fifty percent (50%) by the Writer. Any decision reached by the arbitrator may be appealed pursuant to applicable law.

_____   _____
Writer or Writer's Representative   Publisher's Representative

_____   _____
Date   Date

Section 10

NEGOTIATING E-RIGHTS:

NWU'S RECOMMENDED ELECTRONIC RIGHTS POLICY

The Journalism Division of the National Writers Union recommends that writers be paid a fee commensurate with the original print fee (i.e., First North American Print Rights) for use of a writer's work on the World Wide Web for a period of up to one year. The rationale is that publication on a web site is available to an international audience, which may preclude additional resale revenues for the author. Therefore licensing to a World Wide Web site is similar to first print rights in different geographic regions, i.e., First U.K., First French. Other electronic rights such as CD-ROM and databases shall be negotiated separately at a suggested rate of 30 to 50 percent of the original print fee.

What Does This Mean?

For example, if a writer is paid $1,000 for the print version of her story, she should be paid the same amount for the use of her story for one year on a World Wide Web edition of the publication. She should be paid another $300 to $500 if her story is included as part of a database service such as Magazine Database Plus on CompuServe or at a magazine's electronic location on America Online.

What About Different Electronic Media?

We recognize that different media—such as CD-ROMs, electronic magazines, and archival databases—may yield widely differing revenues for publishers. For example, an electronic edition of a magazine may generate money only from the ads that appear on it, while electronic databases may generate revenue by charging users for each article download. Each of these media represents a different use of the work, and must be paid for separately. This principle of separate payment for each use has long been recognized in print publishing, where rights for reprints, foreign editions, or anthologies are routinely paid for over and above the original print fee.

What About Royalties?

One way to compensate writers for the revenue generated by different media is to pay royalties. A publisher might pay a writer according to the number of "hits" to an article, or pay a portion of a database download fee to the author of an article. The NWU is not opposed to these payment scenarios. But at this time, the largest database operators are unwilling to provide authors with either compensation for, or transaction-based information about, online use of articles. And individual magazine publishers claim they are unprepared to provide a detailed accounting of, and regular payment for, on-line article use. Given these current realities, the NWU recommends that writers get paid a flat fee.

What Are the Advantages of These Recommendations?

At this time, the flat percentage is the best way to ensure you will get paid for your electronic rights. This payment formula does not depend on the honesty of the publisher or the profitability of the electronic venture.

In the future, the NWU remains open to an equitable royalty payment system for electronic rights if publishers can provide accurate and timely accounting and payment to writers.

What are editors saying?
Many publishers insist that because their electronic ventures are currently money losers, they should not have to pay writers for electronic rights. But writers should not be bankrolling speculative electronic publishing ventures by being forced to provide their work for free. Publishers must recognize that the startup costs of electronic publishing include paying writers for their work, in the same way that startup print magazines pay writers long before the publication becomes profitable.

How can I insert this in my contracts?
The NWU suggests you insert the following clause(s) in your contracts if you are licensing your electronic rights:

For a Web Site:
[Publisher] shall pay [Author] $_____ (representing the same amount as the original primary right) for use of the Author's work on _____ [publication's website] for a period of one year. [Also include a license fee for usage in subsequent years or specify that those fees will be negotiated at a later date.]

For Other Electronic Rights Such as CD-ROMs and Databases:
[Publisher] shall pay [Author] $_____ (representing 30 to 50 percent of the original print fee) for use of the Author's work in _____ [one electronic outlet] for a period of one year. [Also include a license fee for usage in subsequent years or specify that those fees will be negotiated at a later date.]

The PRC Exception to NWU Electronic Policy

There will be situations in which writers may be able to deal directly with database services, rather than granting electronic rights to the print publisher. The National Writers Union has negotiated a deal with Uncover, a hybrid on-line fax document delivery service, under which the copyright fees collected by the service will go to freelance writers rather than the publishers. To aid the collection of these fees, the NWU has established the Publications Rights Clearinghouse (PRC). PRC also licenses photocopying rights through Copyright Clearance Center. In the future, the PRC will license electronic rights to other database services or print publishers and will distribute the resulting revenue to freelancers.

If a publisher chooses to license electronic rights to a collection of articles (e.g., the past year's issues of a magazine) through the PRC, writers should allow the PRC to negotiate their best electronic licensing fees. If a publisher insists on licensing e-rights on an article-by-article basis, writers should opt for the NWU recommended fee of 30 to 50 percent per use for the first year and an additional fee per use for each year thereafter.

For more information on the Publication
Rights Clearinghouse contact:

National Writers Union
UAW Local 1981
113 University Pl. 6th Fl.
New York, NY 10003
(212) 254-0279
prc@nwu.org

Section 11

NEGOTIATING E-RIGHTS: HOW TO COUNTER
THE MOST REPEATED CYBERFABLES

DAN CARLINSKY

In the 1930s, two kids just out of high school dreamed up a comic character and sold it to a publisher for $130. Following common practice at the time, the publisher took all rights. The kids were Jerry Siegel and Joe Shuster. The character was Superman.

Today, as traditional publishers and startups big and small ride the shock waves of the electronic explosion, many of us who write freelance articles for publication are acting like those earlier creators who didn't know better, or didn't believe they had the clout to protect themselves. Through our organizations and as individuals, we need to act fast and act smart, lest we become the next generation's objects of bemused pity.

Many traditional publications now have a World Wide Web presence that often includes entire articles lifted from the print edition. Some publishers expect this extra use for free. (For free? Does an advertiser who buys a half-page in a print magazine automatically get a spot on the Web version for free?) For reuse of print material and for works commissioned directly for online use, many publishers want Internet rights to last forever. (Forever? Can a Web advertiser pay a onetime fee and get a banner that stays on the site forever?)

The answer to both these parenthetical questions is "Of course not." Not free because a Web publication is a distinct business enterprise. Not forever because the essence of online is continuing use. Online advertisers pay by the hit or by the time period. Smart photographers and photo agencies generally license online use of images on a timed basis. Writers should do likewise.

An article in a print magazine does its jobs for the publisher—chiefly, helping to sell ads and copies of the magazine—once. An article online serves as long as it's there. Thus, the guiding principle of online publication for freelancers: Continuing use calls for continuing payments. Either a per-hit royalty or a fee per time period works. Accepting a single fee for all time doesn't.

There are several ways print publishers can put articles online.

Thousands of print publications sublicense their content to databases, for which users pay a monthly subscription fee, a fee each time they access an article, or both. Middlemen aggregators and the magazine, newspaper, or newsletter publisher receive regular royalties; the writer, with few exceptions, receives nothing. In another kind of online effort, users can sample articles from various magazines before ordering subscriptions with a few keystrokes; they don't pay for the samples and the publisher receives no royalty, but the promotional value of the extra use of the writer's material is obvious. Reprint services, too, are in the online picture in a broad hybrid setup. Typically, the computer user finds a citation in an online index and orders the text at the keyboard. The pages are faxed or mailed for a service charge plus a "copyright fee." But those payments go to the publishers, who in the case of typical freelance articles don't own the copyright, have no legal standing to collect the money, and were never authorized to make a reprint deal in the first place.

Online and otherwise, secondary uses of articles are booming. Reuse of "content" is no longer a rarity; it's now the rule. Freelancers who give up the right to the continuing aftermarket of their articles are signing away their future.

In today's wagons-in-a-circle climate, it often takes effort for authors to hold onto their rights. It takes work even to understand what authors' rights are and what to do to keep control of them. These days, contracts for freelance articles can be super-dense, high-legalese documents longer than the articles they commission. Rights clauses—in particular, those pertaining to electronic rights—cause the most consternation, especially when the publisher wants those extra rights for free. Often they cause the most confusion, too.

Editors may find themselves called upon to explain and justify to writers a contract that demands for the publisher "the non-exclusive right to exercise, by itself or through third parties, the rights granted herein in any form in which the Work may be published, reproduced, distributed, performed, displayed, or transmitted (including, but not limited to, electronic and optical versions and in any other media now existing or hereafter developed) in whole or in part, whether or not combined with works of others, in perpetuity throughout the universe. . . ."

Editors usually base their pitch to writers on certain basic information about electronic publishing. The problem is, much of that information is wrong.

The Most-Repeated Cyberfables, and What the Freelancer Should Know to Correct Them

"Databases like Lexis-Nexis and Northern Light's 'Special Collection' are just another way we distribute our publication. You wouldn't expect more money if we signed up 1,000 more newsstands, would you?" A database is not simply another means of distributing a publication, because a database doesn't distribute publications at all; it distributes individual articles. It takes articles out of the collective work they originally appeared in and distributes them as part of a new and much larger collective work. It's as if a reader could go to a newsstand that jumbled together the contents of a thousand magazines and newspapers, slice out a single article, and buy that clipping alone. It is, in effect, an electronic delivery system for a reprint service.

"This is just like microfilm." Microfilm, which replaced bound volumes, was a new form of archiving, containing each issue in its entirety, page after page, just as it appeared on paper. But an electronic database—online or on a CD-ROM—is an archive of articles, not of issues. It typically includes articles from different issues of hundreds—even thousands—of publications. Unlike microfilm or back issues on paper, which are sold once and lie on shelves thereafter, today's electronic databases produce a continuing income stream enjoyed by every party in the chain except the author, unless the author-publisher agreement says otherwise.

"We don't charge download fees on our Web site. If we start charging, then we'll pay authors." Download fees are just one of several ways publishers benefit from being online. They gain paper subscriptions and general promotion. They sell ads, products and services, and mailing lists of visitors to the site. In setups with commercial services, like America Online, they may earn finders' fees for bringing new subscribers to the service. Some of the most profitable print publications are controlled-circulation giveaways with heavy advertising; writers don't provide them with free articles just because they don't charge for subscriptions.

"But no publisher is making a dime of profit online." Wrong. With databases, publishers generally have no startup costs, no expenses at all; they sign a deal and royalties start flowing. A publication like the New York Times, which is frequently used for research, already makes millions a year from electronic products. Others make peanuts. But whatever they take in from databases usually is pure profit. On the other hand, publishers' own online efforts, including sites on the Web, may have high startup costs and bring little initial income (although Web advertising is already being tallied at more than a billion dollars a year). But while bottom line is what it's all about, in a print venture no publisher expects profits from day one, and no publisher expects freebies from freelancers. In electronic publishing, before they start turning a profit, publishers quite naturally pay everyone from their computer programmers to the electric company. Why should writers provide content for free?

"We don't know which articles are accessed. It would be too expensive to keep track." Untrue. Some databases and Web publications already do per-article tracking, and a few magazines split database royalties with their outside writers. Regardless, per-hit payment isn't the only way to compensate authors. Continuing, small licensing fees can be reasonable too. The point is: If the article helps make up a product that's used over and over, the writer should keep on earning.

"It would be too expensive to write a lot of small checks." It might be, but writers and agents have joined in the not-for-profit Authors Registry (http://www.authorsregistry.org), which keeps accounts and conglomerates those small amounts for authors. Such major publications as *Cooking Light, Food & Wine, Harper's, The Nation,* and *Travel & Leisure* have already begun to get secondary-use payments to authors via the Registry. "The bookkeeping is difficult, so we'll keep all the money" doesn't fly.

"The exposure will be good for you." By that reasoning, authors shouldn't be paid for print publication either.

"We can't delete just one article." On their own sites, of course, publishers control the content and frequently delete or alter articles first published

in print. Standard database agreements allow the publisher to order removal of any material at any time. Writers can offer publishers a choice: ongoing payments for ongoing use, or leave the story out.

"If you make us delete this article, you'll be interfering with the flow of information, research, scholarship, the future of the world. . . . " In other words, when it comes to aiding research, publishers should be allowed to profit, but authors should perform a public service?

"We ask for only nonexclusive rights; the author can relicense the work too." Should an author have to compete with Condé Nast or Hearst in marketing? And what happens when a potential republisher asks for territory or category exclusivity? The author can't agree, because the original publisher may be licensing those rights to the competition. But even more basic is this question: Should a publisher be able to make continuing use of a freelancer's property and keep all the proceeds? Should freelancers, who are given the right to be intellectual property landlords by copyright law, be demoted to migrant workers by a publisher's decree?

"The business is new. Let it shake down for a few years, then renegotiate." Ever try to push the toothpaste back into the tube? Industry standards of the future are being established now. Publishers and freelancers should build them together. Fairly.

"No other writer has objected." Oldest line in the book of publisher-speak, and rarely true.

"Our lawyer won't allow it." The classic good-guy-bad-guy routine. Best response: "Neither will mine."

Dan Carlinsky is a former Vice President/Contracts of the American Society of Journalists and Authors. Adapted by permission of the author and the ASJA Contracts Committee.

The American Society of Journalists and Authors is the nation's leading organization of independent nonfiction writers, including more than 1,000 freelance writers of magazine and newspaper articles, books, and other forms of nonfiction writing who have met the Society's exacting standards of professional achievement. To all independent writers, ASJA is an influential advocate, speaking out for free-lancers' rights to control and profit from uses of their work in the new media and otherwise. All are welcome to the resources on the Society's Web page (http://www. asja.org) and a free subscription to ASJA Contracts Watch, the widely distributed electronic newsletter (sign-up instructions at http://www.asja.org/cwpage.htm). For membership requirements or an application, see the ASJA Web page or contact the ASJA at asja@asja.org; 1501 Broadway, Suite 302, New York, NY 10036; Tel.: (212) 997-0947.

Section 12

NEGOTIATING ELECTRONIC PAY RATES

TODD PITOCK

In broad terms, there are three types of electronic rights licenses:

- licensing original content to an online publisher;
- licensing online rights to the original print publisher;
- licensing the right to reprint an article online to a separate online publisher.

When it comes to licensing content that has not been previously published, the negotiation is similar to the world of print. As with any market, writers need to become familiar with rates, and they should establish their own floor of prices. That's highly subjective, with some writers refusing to work for less than $1/word, while others need to build a portfolio of clippings.

Consult other writers. The National Writers Union and the ASJA publish information on rates, and the NWU has a database that connects writers who contribute to the same publications. Find out the terms they got. You may be surprised at how much things can vary at the same publication. Don't be afraid to ask up front what a publication pays, and don't be afraid to negotiate. Editors respect professionals, and they understand that professionals, by definition, write for money.

Online publishing does differ from print in a couple of ways. For one thing, Web word counts tend to be low, so even if the word to fee ratio is respectable, the overall fee may not be sufficient. Some writers argue, with justification, that word count–based fees are not a good way to measure value. Still, they remain the industry's method. In addition to their floor of prices, though, writers should ascertain how much work is involved in a project. How many sources does an editor expect to see in a story? Is the editor providing sources? If not, and if the Web publication does not have a well-recognized name, how difficult will it be to reach those sources?

Another difference between online and print publications is the duration of a license. Once, it was understood that a periodical had onetime rights that lasted for as long as the issue was available for sale or distribution. Articles appearing online, though, can stay up on a Web site forever, and some publishers say their most valuable electronic asset is their easy-access index of previously published articles, or what's commonly called an "archive." Unfortunately, the value your article adds to a Web site reduces the value of your article.

If someone can get it online elsewhere, why pay you for it? The answer—and one that's increasingly accepted by online publishers—is a time-limited license. At the expiration of the mutually agreed term—the minimum tends to be a week and the maximum a year—the publisher and writer can renegotiate an appropriate fee if both sides want the article to continue to appear. The NWU's Web zine contract suggests a license that lasts for as long as it takes for a Web site to refresh its main page, i.e., daily, weekly, monthly, etc.

Many print publishers want Web rights at no additional fee. There is, however, a principle to defend and a material reason not to give rights away. The principle is that all of society understands that you pay as you go, and each use deserves a separate fee. The material reason is that there is a growing body of online publications who pay—and well—for online rights. If you give it to X Mag, you can't sell it to Y Mag, and you, the writer, take the loss.

Some writers will say, "Oh, well, I don't have an online market for it anyway." But keep in mind that the online world is burgeoning. What doesn't exist today may well exist tomorrow.

If, on the other hand, you have an online market likely to be interested in a story that already appeared in print, you should use that information when you negotiate. If, say, you're writing a story for X Mag for $1,000 and you know Ymag.com will pay $700 for the online rights, tell the editor of X Mag. At the very least, X Mag should pay a substantially higher fee for an exclusive license and to cover your loss. And remember, in many cases today, online markets are *better* financed and pay more than print publications, particularly newspapers.

Define your contract terms as narrowly as possible. If Fishing.com wants to buy online rights:

a. Get the most money you can. If Fishing.com's fee is not sufficient, see if Fishingrods.com pays more. There may be limits to how much you can cast about, but at the very least, you should know what respective markets pay.

b. Put a time limit on the license. No one should get rights in perpetuity—certainly not unless they pay commensurably for those rights.

c. Define the online market. Sell Fishing.com a three-month license that's exclusive to all fishing-related Web sites.

You won't always get what you want, but you should at least be familiar with, and go for, terms that are most advantageous to you.

Todd Pitock formerly served as the chairperson of the National Writers Union's Journalism Division.

Section 13

SPOTLIGHT: ONLINE EDITOR
. . . .

Debbie Ridpath Ohi, Editor, Inklings, and author,
Writer's Online Marketplace

Inklings (http://www.inkspot.com/inklings, or send e-mail to subscribe@inkspot.com) is a free electronic newsletter for writers and part of the writers' Web resource Inkspot (www.inkspot.com).

Tips for Online Writers

- Most writers don't realize how many online writing opportunities are available to them. Not just writing for zines, but also writing for content-rich sites, electronic newsletters, news and service Web sites, press releases, writing courses, online books . . . and these are just a few. There are also many sources of market information online, places where you can find publisher guidelines and news about the publishing industry as well as job opportunities for writers. I have some listed at: http://www.inkspot.com/market/.

- The Internet has enormous networking and research potential; invest the time to explore the possibilities. Check out newsgroups, discussion mailing lists, online writing groups, and live chats. Learn proper "netiquette" and always read guidelines before posting a message that will be read by many people. If you're surfing the Web for research information, be efficient. Take the time to learn how to properly use several good search engines. Also, don't assume that all information you find online is accurate: always verify the source.

- When querying by e-mail, remember to follow the same rules that you would when sending a regular query. Don't assume that it's okay to be informal just because you're using e-mail. Some editors may be fine with this, but many editors have only recently made the transition from traditional print to electronic media and are still used to traditional methods. In short, be as professional in your electronic communication as you would be in any other form. Also, don't assume that online editors have lower standards than editors of print publications. Send only your best.

- If you're using URLs or specific Internet information in your article (e.g., names of mailing lists, newsgroups), be sure to double-check them before submitting the final copy. Web sites and other Internet-based sources frequently move and disappear, and editors are likely to be unimpressed if they receive an article in which half the URLs prove to be defunct. They're bound to wonder how much other information in your article is also outdated.

SPOTLIGHT: ONLINE WRITER
. . . .

Christina Tourigny

Background

Let's classify my genre as nonfiction—travel, sports, interviews, health, etc. Online: Trips Magazine (http://www.tripsmag.com), Beckett Baseball Card Monthly (http://www.beckett.com), American Visions (http://www.americanvisions.com), Internetwork Publishing (http://www.travelbase.com), Fitnesslink (http://www.fitnesslink.com), Earthlink (http://www.earthlink.com), and many more. Print: *First Books* (travel guide) *Essence, Cigar Lifestyles,* and others.

How Did You Tap Your First Paying Online Market?

I spent days online, finding possible markets with the help of the Email Media site (see "Web Writing Resources Recommended by Online Writers," page 195), and going from one site to the next looking at various writing jobs offered. I applied to all the jobs I qualified for, queried most of the freelance markets, and got my break into online writing as well as several print markets.

Tips on Writing for Online Markets

- You do not have to write online for free. It's your work, and if you want to make writing your livelihood, you need to be paid. If you're trying to build up your credit list then start out with online markets that pay very little and work up—even if it's only a penny or two a word the first few times or maybe $15–$20 for your whole piece. If you build up your credit list with free markets, editors will take notice and offer you a fraction of what you could have gotten or offer you a credit like the others. New writers need to be aware that there are plenty of paying online markets out there for them to break into. Don't just shoot for the big guns. Go after the smaller ones too—they're almost always your bread-and-butter makers. All nonpaying markets have survived this long because new writers are misguided and don't realize they can negotiate with magazines. Don't sell yourself short.

- If you can work with a company that owns, or is hired out by, multiple online publications, it's better than hitting one big market sometimes. I have a lot of regular work from four different companies like this that call me up and ask me to write for them for both online and print (e.g., Beckett's online at http://www.beckett.com). Most of these group publishers don't advertise in writers' markets, so you've got to ask around in newsgroups such as alt.writing, and peruse writing newsletters such as "Working Writer" (call [212] 874-3367 for a sample copy).

▪ Know your rights when it comes to online contracts and be aware there is negotiating room with almost all contracts. National Writers Union (NWU) (http://www.nwu.org/nwu/index.htm) and the American Society of Journalists and Authors (http://www.asja.org) have lots of copyright information. Other sites writers should know about: The Copyright Website (http://www.benedict.com) and Books A To Z Copyright Basics (http://www.booksatoz.com/copyrigh/whatis.htm)

SPOTLIGHT: ONLINE WRITER
* *

Bruce Mirken

Background
News, news features, including gay and lesbian and health.

Online
Gay Financial Network (http://www.gfn.com), San Francisco CitySearch (http://www.citysearch.com). I've done numerous pieces for each—the easiest way to find at least some of them is with a search under my name—though only some of the CitySearch stuff will turn up.

Print
San Francisco Examiner, SF Bay Times, SF Bay Guardian, POZ, many, many, many others.

How Did You Tap Your First Paying Online Market?
I actually am not sure what was my first. Citysearch posted a notice at the Media Alliance, a San Francisco organization for progressive journalists, when they were getting ready to start their SF site, and I answered it with a few clips—just like approaching a new print publication. I think I was referred to GFN by a friend.

Tips on Writing for Online Markets

- Strange as it may seem, I have no particular tips. In my experience, good writing is good writing, and good editors—online or print—will appreciate it. All of the things that print editors appreciate—timeliness, queries that are appropriate for the market you're approaching, etc., etc.—apply here as well. There's no magic bullet.

SPOTLIGHT: ONLINE EDITOR

Alice Bradley, Editor-in-Chief, Charged

Charged (www.charged.com) is the extreme leisure authority. Whether you want to snowboard, breakdance, or wander the streets wearing nothing but oven mitts, Charged will give you the where, when, and how. Our goal is to provide expert advice and information on action sports, urban activities, and unusual travel options. And we're funny, too.

Tips on Writing for Online Markets

- When you're writing for the Web, you have to be hyper-aware of your audience's lack of patience. Think of your text in terms of short bites. Web surfers are allergic to scrolling. Usually when I receive a story, I go through it and see how I can break it up into smallish (eight lines, around) paragraphs—it's just less overwhelming than having a page full of text to scroll through. Often I'm amazed by how much I have to reorganize and rewrite someone else's story. And if I'm not able to spend a lot of time on it, I might not be able to accept it. Putting in subheads is always a good idea. It helps the writer (and the editor/producer) organize the story.

- You should have a general sense of what the design for the story will be. Think of how the text will look on the site. What should be hyperlinked? Should it have simultaneous narratives? A left-side frame with links to specific paragraphs? Could it be a choose-your-own-adventure piece? It obviously depends on what piece you're talking about, but the format should direct your story to some extent. Ideally, you and a producer would determine together what kind of format fits the story, and you would write it accordingly. Long, linear stories will make for a boring design—or a story that has been totally rewritten by an editor.

- Instead of e-mailing clips or URLs with your initial query, it's better just to send your pitch and then offer to send clips, and ask how the editor would like the clips to be sent. Some editors feel strongly about their preferred method, and there's really no set standard. Do you attempt to make nice color printouts of your story and mail them? Do you e-mail attached stories (and then they look terrible because of the HTML, or if you look at them in Netscape, the images are missing), or do you just send URLs? As an editor, I prefer the last alternative; web stories are web stories and should be read as such. But some editors say it's not their job to go looking for your clips at a URL. The only way to know an editor's preference is to ask beforehand.

SPOTLIGHT: ONLINE WRITER

Gary Welz

Background

My writing topics range from advertising and personalities to publishing and technology. Online: Webdeveloper.com (http://www.webdeveloper.com), Crisp (http://www.crispzine.com), and The X Advisor (no longer online). Print: *Internet World, Web Week.*

How Did You Tap Your First Paying Online Market?

My first paid article on the Internet stemmed from my first unpaid article on the Internet. Back in 1994, on the NCSA homepage, I read about an upcoming Web conference that was accepting abstracts for conference papers. They accepted my piece, "Multimedia on the Internet," which they published on their site and were going to present at the conference. I spent $500 to get to the conference, where I had the fortune of meeting the editor of *Internet World* magazine. He ended up paying me $600 to publish my conference paper in the print magazine. When the editor of Internet World's web magazine read the article, he hired me to write a regular online column for $300 a week. Incidentally, that same conference paper was later read online by the editor of X Advisor, who also hired me to write a regular online column for $500 a month.

Tips on Writing for Online Markets

- Although writers need to be compensated accordingly, it can be quite beneficial to have your online articles archived by the publication and available to readers forever. It's even worth setting up your own Web page with your clips and credentials—whether or not you've ever been published online. Print articles run for their month and then that's usually it—they're out of the public eye. But I've received so many opportunities from editors and companies who came across a past online article of mine, or who did an Internet search on a certain subject and my name and article came up—even for articles that I wrote a long time ago. With archived articles, I'm also able to query new online markets with URLs pointing to my previous clips.

- Indulge your loquacity. Yes, some editors prefer your articles to be short, but as long as you can break the writing into short sections, there's no real limit to space in online magazines. They don't have any printing costs. My regular column for Webdeveloper.com had a 600-word minimum. Maximum? Almost anything I wanted. For columns conducive to personality, really let your personality show through.

- If you want to write for the Internet, know what's on the Internet. Search engines are probably the greatest tool for online writers. Search on your topic to see what's already out there so you don't have to reinvent the wheel—and you don't have to submit a story that's already been written. Find source material so you can give it a new perspective. And remember not to rely on just one search engine.

- Get out and meet editors. Sure, you could conduct business entirely through e-mail, but meeting people face-to-face is still extremely important. Build some rapport. Go to events and conferences, and introduce yourself to people. It's a huge advantage to have an editor put a face with your name.

SPOTLIGHT: ONLINE EDITOR
••••••••••••••••••••••••••••••

Melissa Weiner, Managing Editor, Swoon

Swoon (http://www.swoon.com) is the Web's premier relationship site for the twenty-something generation. Swoon is also the online home of *Details, GQ, Mademoiselle,* and *Glamour.*

Tips for Online Writers

■ Investigate each site and pitch accordingly. Don't conduct a mass e-mailing campaign. It's obvious, annoying, and a complete turnoff. Make your pitch site-specific. Keep in mind that every successful online publication provides a unique user experience that your piece should help create. Convince the editor that your idea is vital to his or her site.

■ The Web's interactivity is what distinguishes it from print. For example, you can search for inexpensive airline fares in seconds or check out your investments at a glance. While you are not going to produce a database of inexpensive airline fares or stock market feeds, you can come up with short, interactive, and easy-to-implement features. Depending on the site, quizzes, games, forums, links, or interactive polls might be the way to go. Each content site has its own idea of interactivity and user experience. Keep the value of the Web's immediate return in mind when you are developing your pitches, and determine the focus of the site you are pitching to so your stories fit accordingly.

■ Since a good Web site is not simply an electronic version of your favorite print magazine, coming up with pieces for an online publication requires a different thought process. Take a step back and think about what *you* would go online to read.

SPOTLIGHT: ONLINE EDITOR
••••••••••••••••••••••••••••••

Marisa Bowe, Editor-in-Chief, Word

Word (http://www.word.com) is an intelligent, witty, general-interest publication for men and women in their twenties and thirties that primarily features what we call "creative nonfiction."

Tips on Writing for Online Markets

- Read the site that you want to write for. Online publications often don't fit easily into the traditional categories that print magazines do, so you've really got to dig in and take a look around a Web site to get an idea of what their style is, and what kind of writing they publish.

- Think about the possibilities of the medium. Stories can be nonlinear or hypertextual. They can branch out into multiple narratives. You can incorporate images, audio, animation, or even interactivity. Most writing on the web is no more than material that would work just as well (or better) in print, but this medium has lots of potential that hasn't been explored yet. Feel free to experiment, but don't be surprised if it takes a while to get it right—you can't become a multimedia hypertext virtuoso on the first try.

SPOTLIGHT: ONLINE EDITOR
••••••••••••••••••••••••••••

Joey Anuff, Editor-in-Chief, Suck

Suck (http://www.suck.com) specializes in detonating media myths. The journalistic equivalent of running with scissors, Suck's daily posts are too literate to be called rants, too obsessed with popular culture to be considered academic and too funny to be taken seriously.

Tips on Writing for Online Markets

- In general, home page diaries and hot lists do not make for impressive writing samples.

- The rule of thumb that suggests reading a bit of the publication you're submitting to has not been miraculously suspended for the digital age. The rule of thumb that suggests reading, period, before submitting is also still in full effect.

- Spelling at least one word correctly in your initial query will put you at least one word ahead of the pack.

SPOTLIGHT: ONLINE EDITOR

Noah Robischon, Editor, Time magazine's now-defunct Netley News

The Netley News (www.netlynews.com) covered digital culture.

Tips on Writing for Online Markets
- Include URLs for the proposed story.
- Send queries as the body of an email message—do not send attachments.

SPOTLIGHT: ONLINE EDITOR

*Ellen Ullman, Former Editorial Director, Online Services,
Princeton Review Online*

Princeton Review Online (http://www.review.com), the online division of Princeton Review Publishing, offers information about standardized tests, college and graduate-school admissions, internships, careers, and lots more. Students can find the right college or grad school with our customizable search engines, and they can even determine their chances for acceptance at a variety of schools.

Tips on Writing for Online Markets
- Online writing needs to be snappy and exciting because it's harder to read on computer screens, and I think much harder to retain the information you read. And yes, people can "click off" very easily! So you need to write in a very conversational, friendly, and upbeat way. Use provocative leads, short paragraphs, and lots of subheads to break up the text and make it easier on the eyes.
- Write in first person or about real-life stuff, with sidebars (or links) to fill in the background or related info. For example, I assigned a piece about transferring colleges. The writer interviewed 10 people to get their stories: why they transferred, how they chose a new place, if it was better or worse, etc. His sidebar was the 12 Steps to Transferring Colleges.

SPOTLIGHT: ONLINE EDITOR
••••••••••••••••••••••••••••••••

Geri Anderson

Background

Based in Mexico. Travel. Online: Folksonline (http://www.folksonline.com), Fine Travel (http://www.finetravel.com), Mex Connect (http://www.mexconnect.com), Suite 101.com (http://www.suite101.com). Print: Many newspapers, including *Miami Herald, San Diego News Tribune, Houston Post, Seattle Times, St. Petersburg Times,* and *Fort Lauderdale Sun Sentinel.* Also published in *Entrepreneur, Small Business Opportunities, Sunset, Boca Raton, Travelin', Great Expeditions, Art of the West,* and many other magazines.

How Did You Tap Your First Paying Online Market?

I started writing for free for Lou Bignami of *Fine Travel* ezine, and now he pays freelancers.

Tips on Writing for Online Markets

• Consider writing online as a new business venture. In any new business venture you take a risk and must make an upfront investment. In the case of online freelance writing, the monetary investment is minimal. You need only a kitchen table, computer, and Internet hookup. Your investment will be in time. It takes time to search out the markets and develop relationships with editors, just as it does in print media.

• While the trend in print media is toward smaller, read-on-the-run articles, this is even more the case in online writing. Think and write in byte-size pieces.

SPOTLIGHT: ONLINE EDITOR
••••••••••••••••••••••••••••••••

Jan Grieco

Background

My work has run the gamut from feature articles on Day-Glo golf balls, gnome homes, and ocean dredging operations to travel pieces on the wonders of New England—especially my home state of Maine. As a reporter, I cover state, county, and municipal governments and education and I'm also a pretty good investigative reporter. I make that determination based on the fact that there's usually someone in a municipal or community organization who is mad at me all the time. Clips: Online: L'eggs, Women's In.Site (http://www.leggs.com). Print: I am a regular reporter for the *Forecaster*, a weekly in Falmouth, Maine. I've had print work appear in *NH Profiles*, *NH Spirit*, *ME.*, *Travel Holiday*, *This Week*, and some smaller regional publications.

How Did You Tap Your First Paying Online Market?

Surprisingly, I was invited by the L'eggs editor, who got my name from one of the bulletin board listings. He was specifically looking for women writers for the site.

Tips on Writing for Online Markets

- Write clearly and concisely. I am surprised at how short most online articles are and have found that a bit of a challenge. I've seen some sites with very sloppy, so-called "creative" style. Always follow the KISS rule: Keep It Simple Stupid! I also follow my three-step rule: Tell them what you're going to tell them. Tell them. Tell them what you told them. It doesn't give me as much creativity as with longer print pieces, but I think writing has to be very tight and clean to be effective on the Net.

- Constantly read whatever you can from online publications to learn style and nuance and tricks. That technique isn't much different from scoping out print markets.

- Because it's a little harder to know online readerships and how to tailor a piece to them, writers often need to take a giant leap of faith and trust the editor. I've sat in that seat, so I know not all of them are bad guys (or gals). I also know that it makes both the editor and me happy if we can develop a good working relationship.

SPOTLIGHT: ONLINE WRITER
••••••••••••••••••••••••••••••

Daphne Clair, aka Laurey Bright, Clarissa Garland,
Claire Lorel, Daphne de Jong

Background

Based in New Zealand. Romance is my main focus. I also have published short stories, poetry, short nonfiction, and am looking for a home for a mainstream historical novel. Clips: Online: New Concepts Publishing (http://www.valuu.net/ncp). Print: 50+ romances for Mills & Boon/Harlequin/Silhouette, and Fawcett/Ballantine. Short stories in anthologies in New Zealand including Oxford University Press (some prizewinning), and a forthcoming collection. Poetry in New Zealand and American literary magazines.

How Did You Tap Your First Paying Online Market?

I read about online publishers in writers' print mags, asked for guidelines, and checked out sites. Decided New Concepts Publishing (NCP) looked and acted the most professional. I sent a print manuscript as requested, NCP wrote saying it was as near perfect as makes no difference, thus making me extremely suspicious because it's the kind of thing vanity publishers say. But then they sent me a professional looking contract, a little different from a print-publisher contract. No advance was offered, but they didn't ask me for money either, and they pay royalties of $1 per disk or download sold. (The book is online.) They have rights for a year. Authors choose 3, 6, 9, or 12 months; after that, the rights revert. I was surprised that I was supposed to register and pay for the registration of copyright myself, but they only have rights for up to a year, so I figured that was okay. Later they sent the professionally copy-edited ms., with very few corrections, and got an artist to design the cover for the site and the disk version. When I asked for some advance disk copies in time for a conference here they were airmailed, and although I was prepared to pay the freight, NCP offered to pay half because they had also included some promotional material (that I had requested) for the publisher. As I live in New Zealand, this all cost them quite a bit of money, so I concluded they were bona fide publishers. The art-work is very good. Royalties are paid quarterly. I have received one modest royalty check already, and can expect more. The check arrived in a timely manner and it's certainly faster than any print publisher. The books are published more quickly and the royalties arrive without any six-month time lag as with print publishing.

Tips on Writing for Online Markets

- Only query specifically those markets that seem literate and efficient—ones that provide guidelines and answer mail in a timely fashion—and whose sites look professionally presented.

- Asking other writers how they've fared at a publication can really help. Some sites give writers' e-mail addresses in the bylines.

SPOTLIGHT: ONLINE WRITER
● ●

Deborah Clark

Background

Based in Canada. Lifestyle, humor, adult/erotica, romance, par-enting. Clips: Online: now-defunct, Night Threads (columnist) (http://www.thethread.com), Writing for Dollars! (http://www.awoc.com/wfd.cfm), Inklings (subscribe at http://www.inkspot.com), Windowbox.com (http://www.windowbox.com), Bridges.com (http://www.bridges.com). Print: *Chicago Tribune, Canadian Author, Petite.*

How Did You Tap Your First Paying Online Market?

Inklings was my first paying online market (although I had other articles placed and paid before the Inklings piece came out). I was and am a subscriber to Inklings. When Debbie Ridpath Ohi first became a paying market, I queried her as soon as I read the guidelines. She responded positively and we entered the process which culminated in my article being included in the February 4, 1998, edition of Inklings.

Tips on Writing for Online Markets

- Source your queries. Often queries are culled from a posting (searching for writers), such as Writerswrite or Inkspot. If the information is not included in the original query and the response is delayed or there are scanty guidelines, the slant may be lost. Example: "Hi, I found your posting for a freelance writer on the Arts section of Dallas Today while I was surfing through Inklings today" is more effective than, "Hi, I would like to submit a piece on the upcoming art exhibit in Dallas for your publication." The first example is how I keep track of the who, what, when and where of the sourcing question.

- Employ an accurate tracking system, whether it is PC based or paper (I use a combination). Good records can result in increased sales and reprint marketing.

- Be prepared for an immediate response. It doesn't always happen, but when it does, make sure you can handle the work. If eight queries are sent out in one day and six come back in the affirmative, the writer can be in big trouble if the proposed deadlines, especially if they are new markets, cannot be met.

SPOTLIGHT: ONLINE WRITER
• •

Mike McGonigal

Background
Mostly I write about music—indie-rock, bluegrass, gospel, drone-rock, raw blues, drum and bass, drum and fife, third stream jazz, improv, swinging C&W, folk, Gamelan, minimalist stuff, whatever—and sometimes I write about art—enthused/visionary/self-taught, mostly—and books as well. I have written some confessional sorta things that people have liked, which is cool, and I tried to write comedy but it wasn't very funny. I would like to be an extremely well paid travel writer, or to pretend to be a stereo equipment aficionado, and get sent complimentary stereo stuff—that looks like a swell gig to me. Clips: Online: Word (http://www.word.com), Feed (http://www.feedmag.com), Amazon.com (http://www.amazon.com), Allstarmag news (http://www.cdnow.com), Addicted To Noise (http://www.addict.com), SonicNet (http://www.sonicnet.com). Print: *Village Voice, Artforum, NYPress, Raygun, Spin, CMJ Monthly, Spex* in Germany, *Bounce* in Japan, and *Poliester* in Mexico. One of my pieces, "Junk," was printed in the

Grove Press anthology *Low Rent: The Best of the Portable Lower East Side.*

How Did You Tap Your First Paying Online Market?

The first online place I wrote for was Word. This was when they launched the site. Editor Marisa Bowe knew my writing from the *Portable Lower East Side.* I was asked if it was okay to have my piece "Junk," which is sort of about being addicted to junk food, reprinted online in their first issue.

Tips on Writing for Online Markets

- The problem with e-mail is precisely what's so great about it—its immediacy. I've gotten into trouble with editors by jumping to conclusions and freaking out a bit, sending off a quick e-mail while I was hotheaded, instead of waiting to cool down and send an e-mail asking, "Why is this check for only half of what I thought we'd agreed upon?" or something. I've found that sarcasm rarely works via e-mail. I've found that little misunderstandings can become big things.
- Always save your e-mails that are business correspondence.
- Be clear and concise but not too formal in queries.
- Don't misspell anything in a query letter.
- Don't send too many clips all at once, either via e-mail or snail mail. I usually send book-length amounts of stuff; I think it just confuses people. Get someone else to help edit the selections if you can't narrow it down yourself.
- I tell people to try not to take it personally when they're rejected or their queries are never returned. And if you figure out how to do this, please let me know.
- When you don't hear back from an editor after you've sent them something you've been assigned to do, this is 99 percent of the time a good sign that you've done a sufficient job, and this busy person just doesn't have the time to get back to every writer about every little thing they do.
- Try not to write for any less than ten cents a word, in general. Online, I usually get about twenty cents a word for pieces of all sizes.
- Be really specific and have an idea of exactly what a particu-

lar site needs before sending anything off. I've only had rewrites the few times I dealt with clueless editors who didn't know what they wanted in the first place. This hasn't happened much, but it's bound to happen sometimes, the sheer law of percentage will tell you that.

- Try to divide what you're writing into computer screen–sized chunks; that's what makes the most sense.

- Online editors are always looking for other writers, so turning them on to one good writer will put you in their favor. It is also the best way to get other useful contacts—to swap them with another writer. Not all writers are hip to this, though. Some of them will think of another writer as de facto competition even if you write about totally different things.

- The most important thing is to not take an assignment that you can't do. It feels really cool to turn something down. I turned down a story for a rock magazine that would have involved flying to London, because at the time I had no money for expenses, I was too busy with other stuff and, most important, I didn't much care for the artist so I didn't think I'd do justice to a feature on this person.

SPOTLIGHT: ONLINE WRITER
. . . .
Paul Vee

Background

I usually tell people that I do "odd, brooding autobiographical pieces for a webzine," but I actually consider myself more of a mercenary. I do what people pay me to do and what I like to do. I hope to never get over the thrill of writing, let alone getting paid for what I write. I write stories; I write journalistic pieces; I write copy for corporate Web sites; I write poems; I correspond; I post on electronic BBSs; I write reviews. I like to write. Genre? I like the offbeat and the everyday. Clips: Online: Word (http://www.word.com), MostNY (http://www.mostNY.com), Molson.com (http://www.molson.com/canadian/can.say), otherwise known as simply can.say, GoldenNYC (http://www.goldennyc.com), did a site on AOL called The Dawghouse, and a few big corporate ones that I can't reveal at the moment. Sorry to be mysterious, but they're still being built—endlessly, I might add—and I've signed nondisclosure agreements.

How Did You Tap Your First Paying Online Market?

My first paying gig? Partly luck. It's too long a story to go into the background. Suffice it to say that I wasn't really looking to get into Web writing, or paying writing at all, necessarily, even though I'd written for the corporate world years before and have written a lot in my life. In fact, I think that writers must have the need to write more than even the desire. One must write more than one ought to write. Anyway, I ran into a friend at a party who was editing a Webzine. I told him I was looking for work and he told me that a sister zine needed people. I applied. They didn't want me as an employee, but they told me to submit a story. That eventually didn't pan out, was rejected after the final edit. I had a contract, by the way, with a kill fee, but I never collected it or asked for it in the interests of possible future work. I might do things differently now, but I still believe that one has to be prepared to make all kinds of potential investments in order to make it. These include time, money, sweat, a social life, etc. Anyway, one thing led to another and I submitted some ideas to this friend. He liked some, but he was leaving for bigger and better things and he passed me on to his replacement, who went through the sheaf of stuff and liked a throwaway idea I had sent in. He asked me to write it up. I did. They bought it. Boom.

Tips on Writing for Online Markets

- Never give up. Be persistent. I suppose these apply to any kind of writing and not just the online thing, but the online medium is fast moving and many editors and publishers don't know what they're doing, especially at the higher levels. They'll gamble with something, then drop it a few months later if it doesn't pan out and make them big bucks. Obviously, this ethic has caused a lot of grief because there just isn't a lot of money there now. The medium is here to stay, but it'll be a few years before the advertisers are going to be willing to pay the rates that they must pay elsewhere, and they'll string it out as long as possible before they do.

Writers and "content providers," that odious phrase that the online world often labels us with, tend to be disposable, and if you don't have a thick skin here, as in the rest of the publishing world, it might be best to do something else. My God, I only sermonize this much when I'm really sleep deprived . . .

- Know enough about computers to feel comfortable with sending and receiving e-mail and e-mail attachments.

- Know the medium. Spend lots of time online, whether it be the Web, an online service, corresponding via e-mail, or all of the above. It's important to have bits and bytes flowing through your veins as well as blood.

SPOTLIGHT: ONLINE WRITER
• •

Skip Press

Background
Writing as a career. Clips: Online: Pulp City (http:/www.pulpcity. com), Datecentral.com (http://www.datecentral.com), and many others. Print: *Reader's Digest, Writer's Digest, Boy's Life, Disney Adventures, ComputerEdge.* Books: *How to Write What You Want & Sell What You Write* (Career Press), *Writer's Guide to Hollywood Producers, Directors and Screenwriter's Agents* (Prima Publishing).

How Did You Tap Your First Paying Online Market?
I answered an ad posted in the Writers Forum area of AOL.

Tips on Writing for Online Markets
- Search the Member Directory on America Online, which some people don't know you can do. A keyword screen pops up and you enter "editor" or "producer" or "publisher" and if someone has listed a member profile and those words are in it, you're in touch. I met the editor of my *Writer's Guide* book that way and got a deal two weeks later.

- Get to the point. Know what you're going to say before you start typing. Study the sites thoroughly before your fingers start whacking.

- Search online writer forums (and newsgroups) for ads seeking writers, and respond to them.

SPOTLIGHT: ONLINE WRITER
....

Karen W. Bressler

Background

Fashion, beauty, health, fitness, travel, relationships, local NY, celebrity interviews, etc. Clips: Online: Fashion Window (http://www.fashionwindow.com), Fashion Windows (http://www.fashionwindows.com), TheKnot.com (www.theknot.com); Print: *Condé Nast Traveler, Self, Mademoiselle, Vogue, Seventeen, YM, Cosmopolitan, Elle, Fitness, Condé Nast Women's Sports and Fitness, Bridal Guide, Honeymoon, Elegant Bride, Playgirl, Prevention, Parenting, Beauty Handbook, Fit, Sportswear International, Recommend, The Resident Newspaper, Teen, Time Out NY, Twist,* etc.

How Did You Tap Your First Paying Online Market?

As far as online goes, it's all about networking! The first market I tapped was jewishfamily.com, but that was a spinoff of *Jewish Family and Life* magazine.

Tips on Writing for Online Markets

- There are endless writing possibilities on the Web. Search, search, search. There is so much out there to write. I found this site called www.fashionwindows.com that buys reprints to almost anything fashion related. There's no extra work involved and you get paid pretty decently.

- Know the rights. I was writing for a magazine that sold its online rights to a Web site I was working for. So while previously I was able to sell a similar story twice (I was working for both on a regular basis), now I could only sell the story once to the mag. The site wouldn't buy it since they had the rights to it already.

- Only write the number of words you'll be paid for. People are still new to the Internet and some writers write on and on. The site may print it, but you won't be getting paid what the story's actually worth.

SPOTLIGHT: ONLINE WRITER
· ·
Michael Ray Taylor

Background

Science, nature, and adventure travel. Online: Discovery Channel Online (http://www.discovery.com) and ABCnews.com (http://www.abcnews.com). I also teach magazine and online writing at Henderson State University in Arkadelphia, Arkansas. Print: *Sports Illustrated, Audubon, Reader's Digest, Outside, McCall's, Woman's Day, Writer's Digest.* Books: *Dark Life* (Simon & Schuster, 1999) and *Cave Passages* (Scribner, 1996).

How Did You Tap Your First Paying Online Market?

I had an assignment for the now-defunct Discovery Channel print magazine, *Destination Discovery,* in 1995 when the Discovery Channel Online was launched. One of the print editors making the transition asked if I'd like to try to adapt the print feature, which was on a cave-diving expedition, to the Internet. I said sure, and I've been contributing to Discovery Online ever since.

Tips on Writing for Online Markets

- Strive for a hip, informal style. Online features should read like an e-mail from one interesting person to another.

- Short paragraphs. If you can't see the entire paragraph in a very small onscreen window, it's too long.

- Check all facts. Print magazines often have staff fact-checkers to make sure that you've spelled names right, used the proper job titles, and correctly attributed facts and quotes—but online magazines seldom if ever check up on writers. This means that you're the only one looking out for your professional reputation. Ask every source to spell both first and last names, and never take the word of any single source on a potentially contentious fact.

- Don't give up. I know several editors who admit to having turned down particular writers as many as five or six times before assigning them a feature. If (and only if) your five or six rejected queries were good ideas, well suited to the publication, and professionally presented, the editor may assign the seventh query out of guilt over rejecting the others. Persistence is admired.

SPOTLIGHT: ONLINE WRITER
....

Todd Pitock

Background

General features, essays, and columns on business, travel, politics. Clips: Online: Salon (http://www.salon.com), CNNfn (http://www.cnnfn.com) Interactive, Biztravel.com (http://www.biztravel.com), Jugglezine (http://www.jugglezine.com). Print: *Washington Post,* United's *Hemispheres, Tikkun, New York Times.*

How Did You Tap Your First Paying Online Market?

Back when Biztravel.com was just starting, my friend was an editor, and she asked me to write a few columns. That got me on the Internet, and once I started fishing around, which for a while I did for entertainment, I found other markets.

Tips on Writing for Online Markets

- Don't write for "exposure" on the Internet. You may have other, compelling reasons to contribute for no pay, but exposure shouldn't be one of them. The fact is, the Internet is so vast and so few Webzines have meaningful cachet to offer legitimate exposure. Don't buy the line that a publication isn't making money, so it can't afford to pay you. Webzines have low start-up and production costs compared with print pubs, so they don't have to generate the same level of revenue to be profitable. And it's a strange idea that writers alone should pony up with their work when everyone else involved in a site is being paid.

SPOTLIGHT: ONLINE WRITER
....

JoAnn Greco

Background

Travel, art, and design. Online: Biztravel.com (http://www.biztravel.com), Clubhaven (http://www.clubhaven.com), CNNfn.com (http://www.cnnfn.com), Trip.com (http://www.thetrip.com), Herman miller.com (http://www.hermanmiller.com). Print: *Art & Antiques, Travel Holiday, Ladies Home Journal, Woman's Day, Washington Post,*

Toronto Globe and Mail, Journal of Business Strategy, inflight publication for Delta, United, Continental, USAirways, dozens more newspapers, consumer and trade mags, custom pubs.

How Did You Tap Your First Paying Online Market?

An old editor friend of mine called to tell me that he had been appointed to a start-up Web zine for a new travel site, Biztravel. com. I became a founding subeditor; this was way back in 1995.

Tips on Writing for Online Markets

- Online pubs need copy—they change frequently and also have no writer base since they are new markets. It's much easier to get attention in this field.

- Online copy needs links—links are the foundation of the Web and Web zines appreciate when you provide the links yourself. Also suggestions for graphics.

- Sell only e-rights—this is appropriate and makes it all the more easy to then resell your work to print medium.

SPOTLIGHT: ONLINE WRITER

Patrick J. Kiger

Background

Generalist. Clips: Discovery Channel Online (http://www .discovery.com); British Broadcasting Corporation (http://www .beeb.com). Print: *Gentleman's Quarterly, George, Washington Post Magazine, Philadelphia, Regardie's, Baltimore Magazine.*

How Did You Tap Your First Paying Online Market?

In 1995, I heard through the grapevine that the Discovery Channel was developing a new Web site. Fortunately for me, they subsequently hired an editor with whom I'd worked previously in print magazines. I contacted him and offered my services, and as a result got an assignment to write the first feature ever published by Discovery Channel Online. Since then I've written several dozen articles of various sorts for them, including a number of marquee pieces (most recently, the Panama Canal and Space Entrepreneurs packages).

Tips on Writing for Online Markets

- Work hard to persuade editors that you're flexible and creative enough to handle the frequently outside-the-box demands of online journalism. When Discovery Online sent me and another correspondent to Atlanta to cover the Summer Olympics in 1996, it was really a last-second, low-budget production. We didn't even have press credentials, let alone all the fancy tools that NBC and the other big media operations had—just notebook computers, cell phones, and a couple of cheap digital cameras. No matter. We quickly adapted, filing stories that showed the Olympics from the fan's perspective rather than the press box, and doing stories on the wild, tacky street carnival that the other news media were missing.

- You have to pitch ideas that are going to get their attention, but still fit into the heavily formatted site (and ideally, achieve some sort of synergy with the site's other media). The trick is to suggest something that's synergistic, but sufficiently different that it is strong on its own. I would suggest that when writers study a site where they want to break in, they look at how the site relates to the TV, print, or whatever the sister medium is.

- Make sure you negotiate for an adequate length of time to do the story.

SPOTLIGHT: ONLINE WRITER
••••••••••••••••••••••••••••••

Kimberly Hill

Background

Information technology, financial services, medicine and bio-medical research, freelance writing, writing instruction. Clips: Online: Freelance Writers Guide on About.com (http://free lancewrite.about.com), Columnist on Intraware IT Knowledge Center (http://www.intraware.com/ms/mktg/indaa/itkc/data_mining.html), Instructor for HTML Writers Guild (http://www.hwg.org/services/classes/catalog/b101.html).

How Did You Tap Your First Paying Online Market?

My first exposure to the online world was as communications manager for an online database company, Predicasts, which was then a division of Ziff-Davis. Then, when I became a full-time freelance writer in 1993, I started writing some intranet and online materials for clients I had in my print practice, as part of my ongoing relationship with them. KeyBank was an example of this—I was already writing marketing copy for print materials for them and was asked to develop a set of corresponding materials for their intranet. I expanded my online work by responding to online notices for writers; About.com and Intraware were my first two exclusively online clients (apart from the steady stream of requests from friends and acquaintances to write copy for their Web sites, which I think all of us get).

Tips on Writing for Online Markets

- Know your rights. It's important to have a contract with any publisher, online or print. Draft a letter of agreement you can use in case the online publisher doesn't have one, and have your attorney review it so you can use it as a template. Keep up with the developments in the area of electronic publication rights, and know what rights you're signing away when you submit copy or accept those checks. Your copy is your livelihood, and you are wise to protect it.

- Create community. Get involved in online forums for writers. Some of the best assignment leads will come to you from writer colleagues who pass them along. View other online writers as your support network, not your competition. There's plenty of work out there for us all.

- Spend the time to keep up with technology. Self-training is part of your investment in yourself. Just as you spend hours learning a new writing style or gaining background in a new specialty, so should you put the time it takes into learning about the online world and the software tools you'll need to be competent as an online writer. Learn HTML so you can submit articles in that format; master your e-mail program so you can send binary document attachments and graphics to editors; build a Web site so you can develop an online presence.

SPOTLIGHT: ONLINE WRITER
••••••••••••••••••••••••••••

Angela Eaton

Background

San Francisco Bay Area culture, Web culture, travel. Clips: Online: San Francisco Sidewalk (http://www.sanfrancisco.sidewalk.com), NetGuide Live! (http://www.netguide.com), Preview Travel (http://www.previewtravel.com). Print: *Media Alliance, Dive Travel.*

How Did You Tap Your First Paying Online Market?

I got a full-time writing and editing job at NetGuide Live! while it was in the project stage. They were hiring quickly and I knew the coordinators of the project.

Tips on Writing for Online Markets

- It's extremely important to join some sort of online professional organization for contacts, ideas, and industry information. It sometimes means slogging through 100 e-mails a day, but when you find the gem that gets you the next job it's worth it.

- Also develop enough technical skills or at least language to write for online magazines. The media pundits out there are fairly established so it will be harder to pitch an article on "What Madonna's mommahood means" than it will be to pitch critical evaluations of how to use the newest app.

- Always ask for money even if it's the clip that makes your portfolio. If a publication has advertisers, they can afford to pay you something.

- Know your publications. Thoroughly check them over time before you submit. Research the Web like crazy.

SPOTLIGHT: ONLINE WRITER
••••••••••••••••••••••••••••

Tracy Cooper-Posey

Background

Fiction, primarily historical and contemporary romances, novel length and some short stories. I have had nonfiction published, but it's not my main focus. Online: "The Charlotte Rose," a short story published at Mind's Eye Fiction (http://tale.com). Print: Fiction in *The Western Flyer, The Western Review* Newspaper, *Screams* (Anthology), from WildChild Press. Nonfiction in *Realms Beyond, Connecting Women, Westwrite, Hearts Talk, Women against Violence* (Collected Works). Based in Canada.

How Did You Tap Your First Paying Online Market?

From using search engines, finding sites, and following the submission guidelines—which can be peculiar.

Tips on Writing for Online Markets

- There is no one standard querying and submission process as there is for many print markets. You *have* to read and following the submission guidelines. If in doubt, query first—which can be a fast process via e-mail, and gives you a foot in the door.

- Be polite. Use the same degree of formality in e-mail communications as you do in letters to print editors.

- For the novel-length markets, don't expect to be able to submit your work via e-mail. I know this doesn't make sense, but as they often prefer to read your manuscript in hard copy, they don't want to have to wear the expense of printing off the entire book. So you may find you have to submit hard copy manuscripts for online markets just as you do for print markets. Grin and bear it, is my only advice.

- Learn basic HTML coding—many sites adore you if you can offer your work already coded. Some sites have coding standards—check their guidelines.

- Writing short fiction for online publications requires advanced storytelling techniques. Online readers are far less patient than print readers, who have invested their money up front. Especially, fiction on pay-per-view sites must have intense reader hooks planted in them to draw the reader on. Get to the meat of the story as soon as possible. Don't wander off the point. Keep the reader hooked into the story by whatever techniques you can use—foreshadowing, mystery, unanswered questions, suspense, *anything* that keeps the reader from hitting the Back button.

SPOTLIGHT: ONLINE WRITER
•••••••••••••••••••••••••••••••

June Campbell

Background

Technology, humor, business, profiles, human interest, essays. I also do cartoons—the kind with a one-liner gag. Clips: Online: Discovery Channel Online (http://www.discovery.com), Career Explorer (http://www.careerexplorer.com), Webreference.com (http://www.webreference.com), Folksonline (http://www.folks online.com), and others. Print: I have "regular space" for technology news in *Computer Player* magazine (a regional Canadian computer mag). I have also been published in *Canada Computes, RAM Chowder, BC Agri-Digest, Vancouver Sun, North Shore News, Vocational Rehab Journal, Home Business Guide,* and *Dance International.*

How Did You Tap Your First Paying Online Market?

It was Folksonline. A friend sent me the URL, and I contacted them with a query. They accepted, and I was published online! (And paid!)

Tips on Writing for Online Markets

▪ I find that querying by e-mail is great; it saves me huge amounts of time and money, and I often get replies back much faster than I would using snail mail. Recently, I sent a query to an online version of a well-known print publication. I received a phone call two days later saying they didn't accept queries by e-mail, but would I be interested in doing an assignment for them? I was, and it paid $750.

Online Markets

Section 1

INTRODUCTION TO ONLINE MARKETS

ANTHONY TEDESCO

Online markets are pretty darn winsome right now. Sort of the sweet, bright-eyed siblings of stodgy old print markets. They're fetchingly easy and affordable to approach, forsaking paper, envelopes, and postage for short e-mails with electronic clips attached. And once queried, online markets don't act aloof, gracing you with a response in a few months. They're considerate/able enough to get right back to you within a week or two, often within only a few days. The best part? Despite their empowering allure, most online markets are sheepishly more receptive than print markets. The Internet medium is still so new that there's less competition, fewer writers vying for their attention. Endearing, isn't it? Online markets don't even know how attractive they are.

With such a multitude of markets already online—consumer magazines, corporate sites seeking customer-entertaining content, e-mail newsletters, etc.—you're sure to engage partner publications that share your most idiosyncratic of interests. Just don't be so love smitten that you give away the farm. Or your expensive baubles or, and I guess this is my point, the rights and pay rates you deserve for online freelance material. Negotiate and know that, although we've confidentially included market information from freelance writers when available, many of these listings are solely provided by the market itself. Markets understandably have their best interests in mind when providing their "maximum payment" or their "minimum rights." Markets expect you to negotiate. Do it. Writing is a business. It's unbusinesslike to roll over and play dead freelancer.

Again, and this time in the authoritative voice and actual words of Dan Carlinsky, the former Vice President of Contracts for the American Society of Journalists and Authors:

> Remind people repeatedly that you shouldn't believe everything you read, not even in this book. Contracts are supposed to be negotiable. They aren't orders from the boss. I lean on this so heavily because I see repeatedly that freelancers, especially those who have held staff jobs of any sort (which is probably most—how many people go to freelancing straight out of school?), don't automatically come to this understanding. From childhood, we're pretty much taught the opposite: respect authority, etc. It's hard to turn from that to running a small business, unless someone pounds it into you.

All you need now is a little market listing how-to and then you're ready to go on your merry money-making way.

- The complete market questionnaire that we sent editors and publishers via e-mail is on page 201, for your viewing and referencing pleasure.
- Some markets opted not to complete our questionnaire. We opted to still include them in the book if our sources cited them as having paid for online freelance writing. ("Sources" meaning its freelancers or perhaps its editor who was too busy to fill out the questionnaire but trying to be helpful.) Those listings are shorter/sweeter than most of the book's listings, but still accurate and effective as freelancing contacts.
- All the information was accurate at press time for this book, but online information, like print information, changes. So remember to double-check information and be nice to us. Or at least be helpful—let us know what's wrong and we'll play little violins while we type your change into our free newsletter and notify

every angry reader who purchased the book and signed up (sign up for free updates at http://www.marketsforwriters.com).

- Circulation is not in "hits" (which are meaningless—one person who views one page with 60 links and 20 images registers 80 hits) but instead in "unique visits per month," meaning unique host computers that came to the site in a day (it's the closest gauge out there).

- If an unconventional paying online market didn't fit neatly into our questionnaire format, we didn't force it in. You still reap the full freelancing scoop; just in a slightly more organic format.

- We initially asked markets whether or not they accepted electronic queries. Then we decided that this had to be a prerequisite for getting listed. Hence, we opted not to write "yes, they do accept electronic submissions" in every listing. We also opted not to say, "no, they don't accept simultaneous submissions," or "no, they don't accept previously published submissions." If they do accept those, we said it. If they don't, we didn't.

- When a URL doesn't work: After cursing the Net heavens and notifying us of our error/wanton ways, you might troubleshoot this tragedy by cutting the URL back to its next "/". For example, if "http://www.whine.com/whine/whinywhine.html" doesn't work, try "http://www.whine.com/whine/" and then "http://www.whine .com/". (Then get right back to cursing.)

- Don't say "Aha!" ever, publicly or privately, but especially not when you see our listings for different online publications that are within the same domain (see glossary section for domain name definition, or just take our word for this one). In other words, we've listed Boston Sidewalk separately from New York Sidewalk instead of listing Sidewalk with all of its local publications. They're individual publications with individual contact information and budgets and people doing things. Providing only one listing would be like listing "Condé Nast" as a print market instead of *Details, Mademoiselle, Glamour,* etc. The online world makes it tempting to see markets as "www.ivillage.com" as opposed to "www.ivillage. com/travel" and "www.ivillage.com/pets" because you can get to all the markets from one page. Online publishers are just more able to brand their publications with one publisher domain name.

- We debated which markets should and should not be included. Here's what we went with: In: Markets that are online and pay for original freelance material. Out: Print markets that buy online rights and put your piece on their Web site. In: Online markets that also buy print rights. In, Out, In: Online contests that pay triumphant freelancers, though we're wavering on this one, and didn't get melodramatic about it because only a couple approached us to be featured. Out, In, Out: Technical or copy-writing or corporate writing for Web sites. Very lucrative and wide-spread, but lacking that freelance-writing feel, we think, for now. Oh yeah, a few e-book publishers made it in. They're online and they pay. Seemed apropos.

I think that covers everything. You're officially ready to make the most of our market listings.

Godspeed.

Section 2

TOP 10 PLACES TO BE PUBLISHED ONLINE,

BASED ON PAY AND PRESTIGE

About.com, http://about.com
About.com, 220 East 42nd St., 24th floor, New York, NY 10010. Tel.: (212) 849-2000, fax: (212) 849-2121.

Our very first market listing for you is one that doesn't fit into the neat little market format that you'll find in most of our listings. About.com isn't a normal online market, but sometimes abnormality can be good. As in, $10,000-a-month-to-freelance-writers good. Before you start your spending spree, buying up all those writer amenities such as food and health insurance, know that abnormality may also have its drawbacks. We think About.com's pay and prestige (you/the world might still know it by its former name, The Mining Company) outweighs its drawbacks. But then we don't write for it. Which, of course, may explain why we think of food and health insurance as amenities. Here's the gist: About.com is a network of hundreds of topi-cal Web sites created and maintained by "guides," aka, you. About.com is looking for freelance writers who can write extensively on their topic of choice and then, with the help of About.com, publish their Web-original writing as a regularly updated Web site or "GuideSite." The full freelance scoop can/should be read at http://beaguide.about .com. Interested writers can apply to be guides from links at that Internet address. About.com will respond in two days to two weeks. The rest of About.com's information fits more or less into our format. Established April 1997. Circulation: withheld. Byline given: "Every page of a guide's site has his/her photo and name on it." Rights purchased: "You own the copyrights to all the content and materials created and used by you on the feature and newsletter areas of your About.com site. We own other areas and you give us license to use your copyrighted material on the Internet. We share equally (50/50) in the rights to the commercialization of those sections in other media."

Editorial Needs: About.com covers hundreds of topics in 18 channels: Arts/Literature, Business/Careers, Computing/Technology, Education, Entertainment, Finance/Investing, Games, Health/Fitness, Hobbies, Home/Family, Internet/Online, Kids/Teens, Local, News/ Media, Shopping, Society/Culture, Sports, and Travel.

Payment: Since part of guides' responsibility is to write regular feature articles on their topics, they are not paid for articles specifically. All guides share a portion of 30 percent of About.com's net ad revenues. Guide compensation will be paid out based on traffic to guide sites as a percentage of total traffic on the About.com network of sites. For example, if the traffic on a GuideSite were 3 percent of the total traffic on the About.com network of sites, the guide would receive 3 percent of the 30 percent. In addition, a percentage of About.com's net ad revenues are set aside in a bonus pool that is paid out to guides semiannually. As of press time for this book (but for a limited time, supposedly) each new guide will also be paid a guaranteed $100 minimum monthly stipend against advertising revenues, and About.com is trying to come up with a way to further compensate new guides with stock options (pre-IPO guides received stock). About.com occasionally pays the expenses of writers on assignment.

Advice from Market: "Those interested in being a guide should be familiar with our site, be sure their topic is not already taken and be capable of telling us why they are an expert in this topic area. People should apply for topics they really care about as guides spend at least ten hours a week working on their site."

Advice from Writers: Some writers report that the $100 stipend is actually $100 to $350 a month, "depending on your tenure and quality" and that the top guide does indeed earn about $10,000 a month writing about video game strategies and updating his Guide-Site. The biggest deterrent for freelancers seems to be About.com's noncompete clause. One writer in the Online Writing discussion group (info at http://www.content-exchange.com) says she and most of her colleagues who specialize in a particular topic passed on becoming a guide because, as she put it, "I think it is reasonable to provide original articles to About.com, but not to restrict all your writing on a particular topic to About.com. . . . It wouldn't allow me to write on the same topic for any other online publication or Web site." As a full-time sports consultant, she wasn't in the position to give up consulting on her specialty to become an independent contractor (read: no benefits, etc.) for About.com. Valid point. But one of About.com's guides sums up our overall perspective on writing for them: "It's not for everyone. But I can't think of any other opportunity that would have garnered me this kind of worldwide distribution, marketing, and income all for writing about a topic that I love."

Discovery Channel Online, http://www.discovery.com
Tel.: (301) 986-0444. Andrea Meditch, editorial director.

Discovery Channel Online (aka DCO) is the only market in this top ten list that didn't complete our questionnaire, and the only market I approached during all of my research that didn't respond at all—to three e-mails and two phone calls politely spaced out over nearly two months. We've decided to include them anyway. They do pay well, they do have prestigious name recognition, and they do, apparently, treat writers well. Here's the scoop, compiled strictly from DCO's courteous, punctual freelancers:

E-mail for queries: Andrea Meditch, editorial director, at Andrea_Meditch@discovery.com, or Randy Rieland, executive editor, at Randy_Rieland@discovery.com, or Andrew Cary, managing editor, at Andrew_Cary@discovery.com.

Editorial Needs: One writer says Discovery Channel Online News (4–6 daily news briefs) is a "great opportunity for freelancers" and that it's worth the trouble you may find "trying to get a response." An added perk is that Discovery Channel Online is known for sending its freelancers all over the world for their work. In an interview with Contentious (a Web zine for online writers at http://www.contentious .com), another frequent DCO contributor said he wrote 20 dispatches from the Galapagos Islands, each between 800 and 1200 words, and crafted the serialization into an ongoing interactive storybook presentation about his trip accompanying a group of research scientists. Still another freelancer offers these insights for meeting this market's editorial needs: "Originally, DCO was largely a stand-alone Internet publication, with a lot of content that was totally unrelated to TV. Over the past year or so, however, the site increasingly has become oriented toward supporting the TV channel. They still do original stories, but they're looking for pieces that complement the TV content. One good bit of advice I would give to anybody who wants to write for Discovery: Be familiar with the TV content, particularly the big-hit specials, and try to think of story ideas that might provide some synergy."

Payment: Short pieces are usually around "$1 per word," says one regular freelancer, while one writer cites securing fees "ranging from $500 to the low five figures for a long project that required a lot of travel. Typically, though, most feature articles are in the $1000 to $2500 range. . . . It's very difficult to compare the pay with other print or Internet publications, because assignments sometimes include other types of work, such as helping with the art research, recording sound bites or taking digital photos, or recruiting expert sources for chatrooms. . . . With the exception of an occasional glitch, they pay on time."

Advice from Writers: "A lot of people get the idea that they want to write for DCO, but they're thinking a print-style article rather than a hybrid of text, reader interaction, real-time updating and multimedia, which is what Discovery articles tend to be. You've got to think about packaging, design, how a story could be played visually and in terms of multimedia. You have to pitch something that's going to work on the Web, something that's going to resonate on Yahoo's picks of the week or whatever." Also, "If you're a new writer trying to break into DCO, you have to be extremely persistent. They don't assign a huge number of stories, and they already have a fairly strong stable of writers. You have to pitch ideas that are going to get their attention, but still fit into the heavily formatted site (and ideally, achieve some sort of synergy with the TV channel). Make sure you negotiate for an adequate length of time to do the story, since DCO tends to move rather frenetically at times." Other writers too mentioned the frenetic pace. "It was stressful for me writing up a story in so short a time for only $100 for 700 words. I like having Discovery on my list of publications, though, and they are one of my favorite sites."

Fashion Windows, and its online newsletter, Visuals, http://www.fashionwindows.com
Fashionwindows.com, Inc., P.O. Box 600632, Dallas, TX 75360. Tel: (214) 293-8651/(214) 282-9200, fax: (214) 739-5563. Mari Davis, creative director/webmaster.

"Fashion Windows is an online trade e-zine for visual merchandising and fashion. Its official title is 'Fashion Windows—Fashion thru the eyes of a Visual Merchandiser.' On the Web pages, it is described as: The Internet's database about Visual Merchandising, Fashion Designers and Mannequins." Established June 6, 1997. Forty percent freelance written, but "our future plan is for Fashion Windows to be mostly written by professional writers." Circulation: 50,000. Pays on publication. Byline given. Buys "first time rights, reprint rights; basically, we accept nonexclusive rights to an article and photograph." Accept simultaneous and previously published submissions. Reports in 2 weeks maximum on queries ("usually within a week, but we get swamped sometimes"); one week on manuscripts ("usually two days, but same reason—one week to give ourselves time if we are busy").

E-mail for queries: submissions@fashionwindows.com.

Editorial Needs: Book excerpts, entertainment, essays, fiction, historical, interview, trade. Query. "If it is previously published, the writer can send us the manuscript, [but for] first-time written articles, we prefer queries." Word length for articles: 500–1000 words. "We also accept articles/photo of a store window, wherein we just ask for 2–3 lines about the window, basically, answering the question "Why did the store window catch your eye?" We do the review for the *technical* or trade side, i.e., design flow, the materials used by the window dresser. The 2–3 lines from the writer (submitter) is to show a layman's point of view."

Payment: "Varies. $50 for the store window photo and 2–3 lines of text (see examples at www.fashionwindows.com/windows/) up to a maximum of $1000 for articles and photos combined. For reprint rights, we pay $50 for articles of 500 words or less, $100 for articles between 700 and 1000 words, $200 for articles over 1000 words (usually 1100 and upwards) plus at least one royalty-free photo that we can use in the article (hard to do all text in an article which is that long for the Net)." Fashion Windows does occasionally pay $1/word, but it's very rare. Usually it's willing to negotiate "up to about 40–50 cents per word."

Photos/Art: Freelancers should state availability of photos with submission. Negotiates payment individually. Requires model releases and identification of subjects. Regarding rights purchased: "Fashion Windows only exists online; we tell the submitter that his or her article can be reused on the other parts of the site, such as the main index page (we feature one article per day on the main index page and use a smaller version of the image in the main page). We also tell the submitter that since Visuals is the official newsletter of Fashion Windows and new articles are announced through the newsletter (e-mail newsletter), the photo will also be hyperlinked to the newsletter. It's the hyperlinking nature of the Web page that does it. It's the same article, same URL, but hyperlinked in different areas. We also explain that we have members in our newsletter who only pick up their mail through Telnet and do not have browsers. . . . We send these members hard copies (printed off the Web pages) as a courtesy to them. We have members outside the U.S. who only have access to the Internet through e-mail and university computers. Fashion Windows is listed on university libraries as an industry publication, hence we get a lot of e-mails from students asking to be on our mailing list and asking for hard copies because of their e-mail situation. We inform the submitter that we have to provide hard copies to about 10 percent of our members (we have 1200 members as of this writing). The freelancers who have submitted to us agree to these conditions. If they don't agree, we just don't buy the material from them. Fashion Windows has a responsibility to the membership of the newsletter to provide it to them. We don't charge for hard copies. We shoulder all the cost, including mailing. If our readers cannot see the whole article, we just don't buy it."

Advice from Market: "The easiest actually if you ask me are the store windows. . . . The photograph does not have to be very good. . . . Snapshots are accepted. You can go to a mall, and take pics of store windows. If you want to take pictures inside, you have to ask permission from the store because of security reasons. You can write 2–3 lines about why you like the store window, why it caught your attention. You don't need fashion or visual merchandising expertise because you are a customer. The main reason for store windows is to attract customers. If it caught your eye, then it must be good, huh? I would like to add also that once we work with a writer, we become a steady gig for them. We have writers who send us an article at least once a month. I would like to say that it is because we are nice people. Seriously though, it's because a lot of our writers find it easy to write articles for us because they all go to malls and shopping centers, and find something interesting by just being there. Some of our established writers (those who write for *Vogue, Elle*, etc.) find writing for us less hectic, in the sense that they only write fewer than 500 words. Once they saw their article on the Net, they understood the need for an article to be short and concise. I have also noticed that they tend to serialize on their own, which gives them more time. A good example is a series we are doing about mannequin companies. The writer who is doing it is based in New York and she would write an article for us once a month, doing the interview on her spare time. She was the one who decided to serialize it. So when she sent us the query, we said yes, do it that way. So far, she seems very happy with the arrangement. We sent her a contract for 6 months; deadlines are very flexible because our newsletter comes out weekly and she can choose in which issue during the month she wants her article published. [For the record,] we do not accept pornography, (some people think that fashion is porn), articles that contain libel, are defamatory, or are obscene. Our submission guidelines are at: http://www.fashionwindows.com/advertising/submissions.asp."

Advice from Writers: Writers have been raving about Fashion Windows, describing it as both a receptive market (especially "great for reprints") and a reliable market ("they are true to their word!"). One writer recounts her specific experience: "They particularly liked the 'first person' pieces I wrote from behind the scenes of New York fashion week. So no rewrites here. Although I had to tweak articles to fit them—as in their previous lives my pieces were full of too much British jargon (I write a lot internationally). They pay $200 for reprint articles over 1000 words. If it is an original you have to negotiate a fee. I have not yet written an original piece but expect to get about 50¢ per word. They are based in [Dallas] and enjoy being in contact with a writer in New York who is in the 'thick of things.' They are prompt at answering my e-mails and grateful that I submit on time. I have a good feeling about this group."

Feed, http://www.feedmag.com
225 Lafayette St., Suite 606, New York, NY 10012. Tel.: (212) 343-3510. Steven Johnson, editor-in-chief.

"FEED is a Web-only magazine of culture, politics and technology. We are most frequently compared with magazines like *The New Republic* and *Harper's* and *Wired*. Our contributors range in social and political attitudes from John Perry Barlow and Katha Pollitt to Laura Ingraham and Senator Exon." Established May 1995. Circulation: 250,000. Pays within 60 days after publication. Byline given. Buys electronic and print rights for specified periods of time. Editorial lead time ranges from a week to a month. Accepts simultaneous submissions. Reports in two weeks on queries and manuscripts.

E-mail for queries: editor@feedmag.com.

Editorial Needs: Book excerpts, essays, exposé, general interest, technical, opinion. All submissions should contain writing of high caliber, with thoughtful analysis of relevant ideas. Query, or query with published clips. Word length: 1000–3000. Columns/departments include Daily: (500 words); Essay (1200–2000 words); Deep Read (2200–2800 words); Document (annotation of book passage, graphics, etc.); Dialog (panel members discuss an issue in three rounds of commentary, of at least 300 words each); Interviews; BottomFEEDer (funny interviews with people behind the scenes at well known, often media-related jobs).

Payment: $200–$1300. Sometimes pays expenses of writers on assignment.

Advice from Market: "A query familiar with our format, and our sensibility, is always welcome. Proposals by e-mail are preferred. If you have other work online, please provide the URLs. If you're writing about a well-known cultural, political, or technological phenomenon it is important to have a new take on the subject, to risk being a little offbeat. Ideas for relevant links are helpful, but not at all required. Writing and analysis of the highest caliber is all we ask. No reprints."

Advice from Writers: "[Feed] generally pays me $500 per feature (1200 words and up), and $125 per short item (250–500 words), but the checks tend to come slowly. They have a small, overworked staff, and invoices occasionally get misfiled, etc. Everyone eventually gets paid, though. They pay 50 percent for the stories they resell, but they're also rather flexible about the terms you can negotiate. They do a separate contract for each feature assigned. Tip: Browse the site's archives for awhile before querying—Feed has a specific flavor that comes out better in the aggregate than in any individual piece."

New York Sidewalk, http://www.newyork.sidewalk.com
Microsoft, 825 Eighth Avenue, 18th floor, New York, NY 10019. Tel.: (212) 621-7091, fax: (212) 246-3398. Eighty-five percent freelance written. Kate O'Hara and Dirk Standen, features producers.

"Guide to arts, entertainment, and shopping in New York City." Established May 1997. Circulation: withheld. Pays on acceptance. Byline given. Buys all rights. Editorial lead time 2–3 weeks. Accepts simultaneous submissions. Reports in 1 week on queries and manuscripts.

E-mail for queries: Dirk Standen at dirkst@microsoft.com or Kate O'Hara at kateo@microsoft.com.

E-mail for photos/art: Brian Colby, creative director, at bcolby@microsoft.com.

Editorial Needs: "Reviews/previews of NYC events; word length: 25–100. Columns: What to Buy, Shop Talk, The A-list, City Survival Guide; word length: 75–200. Query with published clips.

Payment: "Flat weekly rate for contributors." Sometimes pays expenses of writers on assignment.

Photos/Art: Send photos with submission. Reviews contact sheets, transparencies, prints. Negotiates payment individually. Captions, model releases, identification of subjects required. Buys all, universal rights.

Advice from Writers: While some writers were quick to jump on the "Sidewalk=Microsoft=Bill Gates=Big Meanie Entrepreneur" bandwagon, some also conceded that Sidewalk is a receptive market for online writers, purchasing 85 percent of its content from freelance writers, one of the highest percentages of any high-profile, paying online magazine. The point of contention is with the rights Microsoft gets with those purchases. The ruckus reached the public eye after the ASJA obtained an internal memo sent to local editors at all the Sidewalk online magazines (New York, Seattle, San Diego, etc.), and printed clips of it in its "Contracts Watch" newsletter. From ASJA's "Contracts Watch": "It seems [Microsoft] has six contracts with different rights arrangements, ranging from work made-for-hire to somewhat limited rights. A page on the contracts' rights clauses explains each and tells editors how to negotiate with freelancers:

> Pick the right contract simple rule: Start with #1 All Rights and work up to #6 Time and/or Product Limited. . . . Use #1 for majority of Sidewalk contributors, especially writers and illustrators, and always for content that gives Sidewalk a strategic advantage. . . . Use #2 if contributor wants print rights to their work and we have no interest in exclusive print rights. . . . Use #4 if contributor insists that MS use content only in specific product(s), if there is little likelihood that MS will use content in other MS products and if content has little syndication value. . . .

The ASJA insists that even the best of the contract deals gives Microsoft "too big an ownership stake in a work, letting the company use and profit from it forever with no further compensation to the writer." They're right. But this criticism also stands for almost every other online publication out there. Microsoft's New York Sidewalk isn't the only online publication trying to gather as many rights and future revenue streams as it can, and it's not the sole keeper of contracts with room for negotiation. One writer's solution: "Make your work as time-specific and Microsoft-specific as possible, or sell them content that has been used for other purposes already. If you think you have a topic that could be turned into a book (e.g., a guide to New York) or used in other media, you can probably negotiate through their boilerplate contracts. But when it comes to stuff with a high market value, you might want to wait before approaching Microsoft." New York Sidewalk didn't respond to this completed listing.

New York Times on the Web, http://www.nytimes.com
The New York Times on the Web, 1120 Ave. of the Americas, New York, NY 10036. Tel.: (212) 597-8023, fax: (212) 597-8001. Bernard Gwertzman, editor. John Haskins, CyberTimes editor.

"[New York Times on the Web] is much the same demographics as the *New York Times* newspaper, highly educated, and upper brackets." Regarding the Times's technology section, John Haskins adds, "Cyber-Times (www.nytimes.com/yr/mo/day/cyber/index.html) is the *New York Times's* interactive daily newspaper of cyberspace, focusing on the social, cultural, political, and economic implications of the Internet." Established January 1996. Twenty percent freelance written. Circulation: 350,000. Pays on publication. Byline given. Buys all world rights, print, and electronic, in perpetuity. Reports in 1 day on queries; 1–3 days on manuscripts.

E-mail for nontechnology queries: Bernard Gwertzman at Begwer @nytimes.com.

E-mail for CyberTimes (technology-related) queries: John Haskins at cybertimes@nytimes.com.

Editorial Needs: News, news features, exposé, interview/profile, historical/nostalgic. "Although New York Times on the Web does buy an occasional piece for the international and arts sections, freelance material is primarily purchased for the subsections within the technology section, CyberTimes." Send query, or query with published clips. Word length for articles: 600–800.

Payment: $400–$500. Pays expenses of writers on assignment.

Photos/Art: State availability of photos with submission. Negotiates payment individually. Captions, identification of subjects required. Buys one-time electronic rights, permanently archived.

Advice from Market: John Haskins explains, "CyberTimes is the interactive daily newspaper of cyberspace. We are looking for features and news articles that place computer and Internet technologies in a human and social context and describe new dimensions of the networked experience, from simple fun to the most serious endeavors in science, politics, and culture." Keep in mind that this is a New York Times publication. CyberTimes adheres to the same journalistic standards and most of the style dictates of the print edition of the newspaper.

Advice from Writers: The biggest allure for this market's freelancers seems to be its prestige and professional editing. Pay is "slightly above average, but not astronomical by any means." One writer who contributes to other sites under the New York Times umbrella reminds writers not to sign the boilerplate contract. "They're open to some negotiation."

Salon, http://www.salon.com
Salon Internet, Inc., 706 Mission St., 2nd floor, San Francisco, CA 94103. Laura Miller, New York editorial director.

"Every day, Salon publishes stories about books, arts, entertainment, politics, and society. Featuring original reviews, interviews, and commentary on topics ranging from technology and travel to parenting and sex." Established November 1995. Fifty percent freelance written. Circulation: 300,000. Pays on publication. Byline given. Purchases exclusive rights for 60 days from the date of the initial publication, unless otherwise negotiated. Editorial lead time varies. Reports on manuscripts in 3 weeks.

E-mail for queries: salon@salon.com.

Editorial Needs: Book excerpts, health, family, academia, humor, personal experience, essays, exposé, interview/profile, religious, general interest, technical, opinion, travel, high-tech, politics, media, news-related, book reviews, music reviews. Word length: 500–2,000. Columns/departments: Wanderlust (travel column); 21st (technology); Media Circus (critical updates); NewsReal (national and international stories). Word length: under 1000. Query with published clips.

Payment: $100–$1000 for assigned articles. Sometimes pays expenses of writers on assignment.

Photos/Art: State availability of photos with submission. Reviews prints. Pays $25–$75/photo. Captions, model releases, identification of subjects required. Buys one-time rights.

Advice from Market: "Submit a query or pitch letter to the general e-mail box. It will be forwarded to the appropriate editor. Additional information on how to query or submit articles is available at www.salon.com/contact/submissions/. For subjects covered, you ought to visit that page on the site and check out the masthead to find out what we publish and who edits it. Salon is in perpetual flux, with new sections starting and others being cut all the time."

Advice from Writers: The consensus is that, as one industry person put it, "Salon is one of the three best sites in terms of content." We agree. Unfortunately, "they're pretty small and not that flush," explains one writer from NWU's database. Most writers report getting paid—or having to push to get paid—40 or 50 cents per word to part with, usually, first electronic rights. Some writers report getting paid as low as 20 cents per word. Another NWU database writer reports payments of $1200, slightly above Salon's "$1000 maximum." Salon is "reluctant to negotiate," explains one writer from the database, though another database writer appends that statement with, "reluctant to negotiate on pay, but able to negotiate contract terms. [The editor] is very open to discussion and will do what he can for you." One writer warns about writing for Salon on spec (which she decided to risk "given their prestige and readership"): "I wrote the story on speculation after receiving an encouraging, but on-spec, go-ahead letter from the editor. I called him after waiting about a month and discussed the story with him, and he was completely enthusiastic about the subject, but said he is overwhelmed with his workload and had yet to open the my envelope. The story includes high-quality photography. It's been about 2 months with no word yet." It seems, though, that the aforementioned lapse in editorial consideration is more the exception than the norm. One writer reports that Salon pays promptly, "generally within two weeks, and I've never had to call anyone to ask where my check was." His tip for writers: "Be patient, and don't try to rush the editorial process. They have a lot of content to deal with, and sometimes it takes a week or so to get an e-mail answered, or a draft read." And occasionally it takes less. One writer reports that he followed the "very simple and clear guidelines on the site, e-mailed the appropriate person (in the Tech section in this case) and heard back within an hour." Even though this writer wasn't ecstatic about Salon's pay rate, he made it clear that "the people I dealt with were great . . . overall they get the thumbs up in my book." (In ours, too.)

The Wall Street Journal Interactive Edition, Interactive Journal, http:// wsj.com

Dow Jones & Co., 200 Liberty St., New York, NY 10281. Tel.: (212) 416-4750, fax: (212) 416-3548. Rich Jaroslovsky, managing editor.

"The online edition of the *Wall Street Journal* is the most successful paid news and information site on the Internet. The Interactive Journal features updated business and worldwide news 24 hours a day, seven days a week." Established April 1996. Five percent freelance written. Circulation: 285,000 paid subscribers. Pays on publication. Byline given. Buys rights for online publication. Reports in two weeks on queries and manuscripts.

E-mail for queries: editors@interactive.wsj.com.

Editorial Needs: How-to, interview, new product, technical, technology, trade, travel. Query.

Payment: "Negotiable." Sometimes pays the expenses of writers on assignment.

Photos/Art: State availability of photos with submission. Negotiates payment individually. Requires captions and identification of subjects.

Advice from Writers: WSJ has that same prestige cachet as its print counterpart. Writers seeking prestige report that they are willing to take the good with the bad. "Pay rates are lousy," says one writer. "For an 800- to 1200-word article you are paid just $300." She then points out, though, "The flip side is that the editors (at least the one I worked with) was kind, efficient, and professional." WSJ publisher Dow Jones Interactive has been commended as one high-profile publisher that truly is "kind, efficient, and professional." ASJA's "Contracts Watch" newsletter reported that "an editor at *Context*, a business-and-technology magazine, granted a request from Dow Jones Interactive to post a freelancer's article on a DJI company-only Web page. Three days later, another *Context* editor noted that the magazine didn't own the rights and informed DJI. The writer finishes the story:

> Dow Jones not only took it off immediately, but also contacted me and offered to pay for a mistake that wasn't even theirs. I got a letter of apology and a $300 check, $100 for every day the story was up. Since it was an inside site, I would never have known of the infraction if they hadn't called me. It makes me think that there might be some reasonable people in the online publishing community after

all, and it makes me all the more convinced of the need for free-lancers to control their electronic rights.

Women.com, http://www.women.com
Women.Com Networks, Inc., 1820 Gateway Dr., Suite 100, San Mateo, CA 94404. Lisa Stone, director of programming.

"Women.com is a leading network for women. It includes 20 chan-nels, including Career, Entertainment, Money, Small Business, Travel, Weddings, plus 12 magazine sites, including *Cosmopolitan, Redbook,* and *Prevention.* Updated daily. Established August 1995. Thirty percent freelance written. Circulation: 4 million. Pays on acceptance. Byline given sometimes. Buys all rights. Editorial lead time is 1–3 months. Reports in a few weeks on queries.

E-mail for queries: editor@women.com. "Unsolicited manuscripts not accepted."

Editorial Needs: Personal experience (first-person Op-Eds), essays, interview/profile (female movers and shakers, celebrity and other-wise), general interest (features). No long articles wanted. Query with published clips. Word length for articles: 300–1000 words.

Payment: "Negotiates payment individually."

Advice from Market: "Be sure to visit Women.com at http://www.women.com before you make any queries. See what kinds of things are featured already. When pitching an idea, make Web-specific sugges-tions, i.e., about how you'd lay it out or illustrate it, how it's interactive. Think very visually about your piece. Note that unsolicited manu-scripts are not accepted. And note that Women.com is flooded with inquiries; editors look for published writers who have written for national publications and who have Web experience, great clips, and original ideas."

Advice from Writers: One writer from NWU's database reports Women.com being very open to negotiating. This writer was able to parlay the rate up to $2 per word, a rate already high enough that part-ing with "all rights, with no additional compensation" seemed fine. Another writer reports having "a very good experience" with Women.com, in that "they were very receptive to pitches and basically very friendly, professional, encouraging etc., throughout the whole process of working on and revising the piece. They also paid me fairly and promptly (and were open to negotiation, though I didn't negotiate much)." That writer also noted an apparently temporary downside to writing for Women.com. "They never actually published my piece because the editor I was working with quit right after I delivered the piece and then gave it to another editor who (though also nice over the phone) basically didn't know what to do with it. She was encouraging me, however, to pitch more story ideas. The only reason I haven't followed up on it is that I feel that their editorial department is quite disorganized. They seem to be in a state of transition, and I'm sure that writers will have a better experience working with them once things have settled down a bit more (I know they recently got bought by another company). My tip for writers who wish to pitch to Women.com is to figure out what section of the site they want to write for and simply [contact] the editor of that section."

Word, http://www.word.com

Zap Corp., 1700 Broadway, 9th floor, New York, NY 10019. Michelle Golden, managing editor. Eighty percent freelance written.

"Word is an intelligent, witty, general-interest publication for men and women in their twenties and thirties that features primarily what we call 'creative nonfiction.' Word doesn't publish reviews, celebrity or lifestyle stories, or anything self-consciously trendy. Word does publish irreverent and insightful personal essays and eccentric humor pieces." Established July 1995. Circulation: 80,000. Pays on acceptance. Byline given. Buys exclusive electronic rights for 60 days, nonexclusive thereafter. Editorial lead time varies, but generally 1–3 months. Accepts simultaneous submissions and previously published submissions. Reports in 2 weeks on queries; 4–6 weeks on manuscripts.

E-mail for queries: word_editor@word.com.

Editorial Needs: Book excerpts, humor, personal experience, essays, inspirational, photo feature, exposé, interview/profile, religious, general interest, historical/nostalgic, opinion, travel. "We *do not want* straight journalism, reviews, celebrity stories, stories about the media, product reviews, or stories about the Internet or digital media. Columns: Work (people talking about their jobs); Money (real-life situations involving the drama of money); both 1,500 words. We only publish fiction by well-known writers." Query, query with published clips, or send complete manuscript. Word length for articles: 400–3000.

Payment: Pays $200–$1500 for assigned articles; $100–$1000 for unsolicited articles.

Photos/Art: State availability of photos with submission. Reviews contact sheets. Negotiates payment individually. Buys exclusive electronic rights for 60 days, nonexclusive thereafter.

Advice from Market: "For aspiring Word writers, we have two pieces of advice: (1) Read the magazine before you submit a query, and (2) Don't write in a typical, glib, "professional" magazine voice—we hate that. Word has a very particular voice, and many different subject areas are permissible, as long as they're written in the right kind of voice. Written material is best submitted through e-mail or on disk (but note that disks or hard copy cannot be returned). Please try to keep text submissions under 2000 words. Photos, video and audio cassettes, and other art pieces should include a stamped, self-addressed envelope if you want us to return them. Our official submissions page is at http://www.word.com/info/submit.html."

Advice from Writers: Word is consistently praised by writers as one of the best online markets to work with. They pay well, they pay on time, and they really get into the stories which, according to one writer, "makes all the difference." One writer did express disappointment, however, explaining that Word had "a bad contract and won't make changes—and they pay poorly to boot." That writer knows contracts and frequently gets paid $1–$2 per word for his online writing. Another writer too expressed disappointment, stating that Word had someone else record the audio version of his story. But he still insisted: "It's been swell to work for them, they are a classy operation, and I've really enjoyed working with my editor." Word seems to be most receptive to personal writing. "You should be the main character in the piece, not outside it," explained one writer. And don't forget to heed Word's preference for e-mail submissions. One writer got his break into online writing by mailing (snail mail) a hard-copy manuscript to Word, but he had to wait nine months for a reply.

Section 3

ONLINE MARKET DATABASE: SUBMISSION GUIDELINES AND PAY AND POLICY INFORMATION ON OVER 200 ONLINE MARKETS

ABCNEWS.com, http://www.abcnews.com
ABCNEWS.com, 7 West 66th St., 3rd floor, New York, NY 10023. Tel.: (212) 456-2225, fax: (212) 579-7914. Mary Bruno, executive producer.

"ABCNEWS.com is the fastest-growing news site on the Internet. The best way for writers at large to regard us is as a major daily national and international newspaper. We often use stringers for breaking news." Established May 1997. Five percent freelance written. Circulation withheld. Byline given. Buys international rights. "No unsolicited manuscripts; they will be deleted upon arrival."

E-mail for national breaking-news queries: Ana Benshoff, national desk editor, at benshoa@abcnews.com.

E-mail for foreign breaking-news queries: Dorian Benkoil, foreign desk editor, at benkoid@abcnews.com.

E-mail for general queries: Beau Brendler, managing producer, New York, at brendlb@abcnews.com.

Phone number for queries to Rose Pike, health editor, (425) 468-4000.

Phone number for queries to Mark Bryant, science editor, (425) 468-4000.

Phone number for queries to Jill Hodges, travel editor, (425) 468-4000.

Phone number for queries to Richard Martin, technology editor, (425) 468-4000.

Phone number for queries to Adam Glenn, business editor, (212) 456-2225.

Editorial Needs: Exposé, general interest, technology, travel. Query by e-mail only. Word length for articles: 500 for news, negotiable for features.

Payment for assigned articles: $150–$400. Sometimes pays the expenses of writers on assignment.

Photos/Art: State availability of photos with submission. Negotiates payment individually. Requires captions and identification of subjects. Buys onetime rights.

Advice from Market: "No new product announcements from technology companies. Before pitching stories to foreign or national desks, try to imagine whether the story would appear on the evening news or in the A section of a major national U.S. daily newspaper." New writers have a better chance of writing for the section editors as opposed to the breaking-news editors because there's a longer cycle for pieces.

ACI (Academic Consulting International), http://www.aci-plus.com
ACI, P.O. Box 4489, Foster City, CA 94404. Dan Berman, editor.

"ACI is a service, rather than a publication. . . . a San Francisco Bay Area–based company providing educationally related consulting, research, and editorial services to a largely foreign clientele, including students, faculty, and administrators. We use freelance writers entirely."

E-mail: Instead of querying him via e-mail, Dan asks freelancers to first read his market's freelancing details available online at http://www.aci-plus.com/jobs/. Again, "No over-the-transom [i.e., via e-mail] freelance submissions." E-mail contact information is available at the site after perusing the guidelines.

Editorial Needs: "Numerous institutions of higher learning, many of them U.S.-based, are in the process of establishing English-language degree programs in non-English-speaking countries, many of them in Asia. Much of the workload for which additional (work-from-your-own-home) writers currently are needed involves the production of 'models' to be used in these educational programs, to provide standards and examples for students to follow. The subject matter we cover, therefore, runs the entire gamut of topics one encounters at the college and graduate school levels. For the most part, however, the work we do is concentrated in the domains of business, humanities, and social sciences. (We also need editors, although there is less of a demand for pure editing as opposed to editing and writing in combination.) . . . If you are well-versed in accounting, computer programming, economics, engineering (any aspect), finance, mathematics (including statistics), or any of the physical sciences, you are especially encouraged to contact us. (These fields typically offer higher compensation than most others.)"

Payment: "For ACI, the average pay is $40 per page (250 words), with a minimum job fee of $250. Writers with whom we have established close working relationships make $2000 to $3000 monthly—in some cases even more—from the work they do for us. (Please note that this does not constitute any promise or guarantee of income.) These are top-notch pros, with ready access to all necessary resources and capable of working quickly, who do other work as well. We discourage writers from becoming dependent upon us as their exclusive source of income."

Addicted To Noise, http://www.addict.com
SonicNet, Inc., 375 Alabama St., Suite 480, San Francisco, CA 94110. Please mail queries and samples of your work. Do not call or fax. Michael Goldberg, SonicNet editorial director/Addicted To Noise editor in chief.

"Addicted To Noise is a new music magazine that covers rock, hip-hop, electronic, and various other more esoteric musics. We run in-depth interviews with artists, columns by name music journalists, new artist features. Most interviews include audio interview excerpts, video clips of the artist, and original photos. Columns and 25 percent of our features are written by freelance writers." Established December 1994. Circulation: withheld. "Portions of our editorial content reaches tens of millions of music fans each month. We provide headline music news to The Box music television channel, which can be accessed in over 30 million homes. Radio and print media also make use of some of our content. Portions of our content also appear on third-party Web sites in the U.S. and abroad." Pays on publication—currently checks go out 4 to 6 weeks after publication. Byline given. Buys all rights in all media. "We are only interested in original material that has never been published before, and it must conform to our very specific standards." On queries and manuscripts: "If we're interested, you'll hear from us. If not, you won't."

E-mail for queries: Lisa@sonicnet.com.

Editorial Needs: Book excerpts occasionally, exposé, interview, music. Query with published clips. Word length for articles: Q&A/features: 1500–4000.

Payment: Negotiates payment individually. Minimal expenses covered on occasion.

Photos/Art: State availability of photos with submission. Negotiates payment individually. Buys all online rights.

Advice from Market: "Study our music news, album reviews, and Addicted To Noise interviews and features. We are looking for writers who can deliver the kind of editorial that you will find in abundance on the Web sites."

Albumreviews.com, http://www.albumreviews.com
SonicNet, Inc., 375 Alabama St., Suite 480, San Francisco, CA 94110. Please mail queries and samples of your work. Do not call or fax. Michael Goldberg, SonicNet editorial director/Addicted To Noise editor in chief.

"Albumreviews.com is our album review area where we focus on new music in the rock, hip-hop, pop, dance, electronic, and alternative genres. Ninety percent of our album reviews are written by freelance writers." Established December 1994. Circulation: withheld. "Portions of our editorial content reaches tens of millions of music fans each month. We provide headline music news to The Box music television channel, which can be accessed in over 30 million homes. Radio and print media also make use of some of our content. Portions of our content also appear on third-party Web sites in the U.S. and abroad." Pays on publication—currently checks go out 4 to 6 weeks after publication. Byline given. Buys all rights in all media. "We are only interested in original material that has never been published before, and it must conform to our very specific standards." On queries and manuscripts: "If we're interested, you'll hear from us. If not, you won't."

E-mail for queries: Lisa@sonicnet.com.

Editorial Needs: Music, specifically album reviews. Query with published clips. Word length for articles: 300–350.

Payment: Negotiates payment individually. Minimal expenses covered on occasion.

Photos/Art: State availability of photos with submission. Negotiates payment individually. Buys all online rights.

Advice from Market: "Study our music news, album reviews and Addicted To Noise interviews and features. We are looking for writers who can deliver the kind of editorial that you will find in abundance on the Web sites."

Alexandria Digital Literature, http://www.alexlit.com
Kathy Ice, executive editor.

Kathy explained that Alexandria Digital Literature is more like an e-book publisher, "not a magazine. We publish and sell fiction works on an 'a la carte' basis." Peruse the site and query before submitting.

E-mail for queries: Kathy Ice at kice@alexlit.com.

Alley Cat News Online, http://www.alleycatnews.com
Alley Cat News says it's the leading publication covering the business behind Internet and technology companies in New York and the tri-state area. They have regular features on companies looking for funding and also provide information on how to tap capital resources. Peruse the site and query before submitting.

E-mail for queries: Editor Julie Jarema at editor@alleycatnews.com or editor in chief Anna Wheatley at acwheatley@alleycatnews.com.

All Health, http://www.allhealth.com
iVillage: The Women's Network, 170 Fifth Avenue, New York, NY 10010. Fax: (212) 604-9133. Kellie Krumplitsch, editorial director.

All Health (formerly BetterHealth) cites itself as "Information you need. Community you trust," covering the full gamut of health—prevention strategies, alternative solutions, traditional medicine, and home-remedy options. Columns and features range from trouble-shooting hot flashes to back pain, and picking over the age-old question of red wine as elixir.

E-mail for queries: Sally Jones at sallyjones@mail.ivillage.com.

[For full listing see Parent Soup on page 157.]

Allmovie.com, http://www.allmovie.com
AMG—All-Media Guide, 301 E. Liberty, Suite 400, Ann Arbor, MI 48104. Darcel Rockett, editor.

This book's senior contributing writer Karen Morrissey explains, "All-Movie Guide is a market for essays, interviews, and other movie news—with translations to six languages." As cited in the Writers List discussion group (info at http://www.perton.com), editor Darcel Rockett needs "freelancers—not reviewers necessarily—but people who can write about the movies, because they love them so much. . . . Everything and anything about movies is what this e-zine is all about." Peruse the site and query before submitting.

E-mail for queries: "Ideas and queries are highly encouraged. . . . have them reach me at darroc@allmovie.com or send ideas [via regular mail to the address above].

Editorial Needs: "We're looking for pieces that could fit in either Movieline or Film Comment—the light with the heavy. . . . Specifically anyone who can write informative, engaging analytical, humor, or feature articles on movie trends, genres, directors, actors, obscure films, or just the movie industry in general."

Payment: Varies, but Darcel Rockett assures "yes, we pay."

All Politics, http://www.cnn.com/allpolitics
This CNN news site is all politics. Not some politics. Not primarily politics. Not 99 percent politics. All politics. Send queries to: Interactive Producer, Assignment Desk, All Politics, One CNN Center, P.O. Box 105366, Atlanta, GA 30348.

[For full listing see CNN.com on page 111.]

All-Story Extra, http://www.zoetrope-stories.com/extra/index.html
As reported from http://www.writersmarkets.com: Zoetrope. Mare Freed and Jim Nichols, editorial coordinators.

"Created by Francis Ford Coppola, All-Story Extra is a monthly online supplement to Zoetrope All-Story featuring outstanding new literary fiction by emerging and established authors." One hundred percent freelance. Pays on publication. Buys first N.A. serial rights and first negotiation/last refusal rights (pertains to film, television, video bidding rights). Responds 1–6 months.

Editorial Needs: "Literary and mainstream fiction, no (specific) genre, up to 7,000 words. Highest quality writing, emerging and established writers, absolutely no first drafts or poorly crafted work.

Submit online via the Zoetrope workshop only at http://work shop.fcoppola.com. No e-mail submissions accepted.

Payment: Pays $100 per published story.

Advice from Market: "Submit your very best and read the publication. Our back issues give the most accurate picture of what we publish. Sample free at Web site. Subscription free. Guidelines at the Zoetrope free online workshop, http://workshop.fcoppola.com."

Altair Magazine, http://www.sfsite.com/altair
Altair Publishing, P.O. Box 475, Blackwood, SA 5051 Australia. Tel.: 61-8-8278-8995, fax: 61-8-8278-5585. Robert N. Stephenson, editor.

Altair Magazine describes itself as "mainly science fiction and fantasy short stories and articles." One hundred percent freelance written. Established January 1997. Circulation: 200 unique visits per month. Byline sometimes given. Buys first English world rights. Reports on manuscripts in 4–5 weeks.

E-mail (for queries only—manuscripts must be mailed): altair@ senet.com.au.

Editorial Needs: Fiction. Word length for stories: up to 10,000. Send complete manuscript with SASE—either 1 IRC (or US$1) for business envelope return, or 4 IRCs (or US$5) for manuscript return. E-mail responses also available (no SASE required).

Payment: 3 cents/word up to $250. Pays on acceptance.

Amazon.com, http://www.amazon.com
Amazon.com is that punchy little online bookseller that could. In the face of traditional bookselling behemoths, Amazon pioneered e-commerce, won over Wall Street, and became so successful selling books online that it's since moved on to videos, CDs, auctioned goods, and who-knows-what next week. We're fans, despite feeling slightly jilted—Amazon's editorial department didn't complete our nifty survey. Peruse the site and query before submitting.

E-mail for queries: Editorial director Katherine Koberg at kkoberg @amazon.com.

Advice from Market: "We're a retailer, not a publication, and accordingly we never accept submissions. When we need contributors we post the openings on our site. If writers send in resumes and clips, whether for a job or freelance, they end up in our recruiting department, where they usually await being matched up with an open job. All book excerpts come directly from publishers at no cost, as do images and author photos, so there's very little that we need."

Advice from Writers: Despite its stance above, some freelancers say Amazon.com does purchase its share of content. One writer in NWU's database enjoyed 50 cents/word for "a monthly gig doing book reviews, articles, and personalized e-mails to subscribers about interesting new books in my subject area." That writer also stated that Amazon.com editors are "very open" to content ideas, but "less so as to money."

American Demographics, http://www.demographics.com
Intertec Publishing, 11 River Bend Dr. South, Stamford, CT 06907. Tel.: (203) 358-9900, fax: (203) 358-5823. John McManus, editor.

American Demographics caters to "business leaders," covering consumer trends, tactics and tips for marketers, the full gamut of marketing conferences and trade shows, and business forecasts based on demographic trends.

E-mail for queries: john_mcmanus@intertec.com.

[For full listing see Catalog Age on page 106.]

AndoverNews, http://www.AndoverNews.com
Andover Advanced Technologies, 50 Nagog Park Rd., 2nd floor, Acton, MA 01720. Tel.: (978) 635-5300, fax: (978) 635-5326. Robin Miller, senior editor.

This market describes itself as "Totally geek! [The AndoverNet network of sites is] the online equivalent of a trade magazine publisher that focuses purely on computer hardware and software, webmastering, and IT management." Topics of AndoverNews specifically include online advertising, e-commerce, and processors, as well as many other related technology subjects. News is often pulled from the likely sources, i.e., the Associated Press, the PR Newswire, and the Business Wire. Current technology news as well as personal reviews on products and technology subjects are also present throughout the site. Established 1997. Seventy percent freelance written. Circulation: 12 million (across 22 domains). "Andover.Net purchases freelance writing as a network, not site by site." Peruse www.andover.net for its growing number of sites and current URLs before querying. Byline given sometimes.

E-mail for queries: robin.miller@andover.net.

Editorial Needs: Technical, technology. Peruse site for nuances before querying.

Payment: "We pay generously, generally by the week or month rather than per word or article."

Advice from Market: "Andover does not accept onetime submissions. All of our freelancers work under long-term contracts. We currently do not need photos, but this may change. Please query only if you are interested in long-term contract assignments if/when we have openings, and only if you can write coherently on computerish topics for an audience composed of skilled programmers, hackers, and webmasters. Location is not a barrier; we currently have active telecommuters in six U.S. states."

Animation Express, http://www.hotwired.com/animation
Wired Digital, 660 3rd St., 4th floor, San Francisco, CA 94107. Tel.: (415) 276-8400.

Animation Express is a how-to haven for Internet animation. Most of the features, which are basically movie shorts, are created using software like Flash and Director. And luckily for those of us who aren't fluent in the latest Director lingo, they provide in-depth tutorials covering all aspects of the web animation process. This market didn't complete our questionnaire, but confirmed that it buys online freelance material. Peruse the site and query before submitting.

E-mail for queries: Craig Schwartz at shvatz@wired.com

Anotherealm, http://anotherealm.com
Anotherealm, 287 Gano Ave., Orange Park, FL 32073. Tel.: (904) 269-5429. Jean Goldstrom, editor.

One hundred percent freelance written. "We publish science fiction, fantasy and horror stories, up to 5000 words maximum." Established September 1998. Circulation: 1600. Pays on acceptance. Byline given. Buys onetime electronic publication and option for possible inclusion in an Anotherealm anthology. Sometimes accepts previously published work. Reports in 60 days on manuscripts.

E-mail for submissions: goldstrm@tu.infi.net

Editorial Needs: Fiction. Send complete manuscript. Word length for stories: maximum 5000.

Payment: $5.

Advice from Market: "We have writers' guidelines available on the Anotherealm site."

Anti-Social Magazine, http://www.antisocial.cjb.net
Tel.: (44) 0797-033-2378. Armageddon, editor.

This market describes itself as "a magazine covering every scene of the underground, from hacking and phreaking right through to the latest news and reviews in the rave scenes. This is currently the UK's most-read underground e-zine, [with] over 35,000 readers globally a month." Rarely works with new writers. Circulation: withheld. Distributed through numerous Web sites. Buys first rights. No reprints. Responds to queries and manuscripts in 4–10 hours. Sample at Web site. Subscription free via e-mail. Guidelines by e-mail and in every issue of the magazine. Thirty percent freelance written.

E-mail for queries: armageddon@hack-net.com.

Editorial Needs: "Pirate radio and system security (NT or UNIX) articles." Articles must not exceed 28K. Submit query or complete manuscript by e-mail to anyone on their staff.

Payment: Revenues from each issue are distributed to contributing writers of that issue.

Advice from Market: "Submission format: we only accept [text-only files], as it's the most flexible from one system to another. Too many people try and submit in Word. Writers should write about scenes they specialize in. If they don't, the end result often comes out very dry and not as interesting for the reader."

Aquent Magazine, http://www.aquent.com
Aquent, 711 Boylston St., Boston, MA 02116. Tel.: (617) 535-5086, fax: (617) 535-5003. Lawrence San, editorial and creative director.

Ninety percent freelance written. "Aquent.com is a colorful, mildly irreverent online magazine for and about independent professionals. It's the magazine for boss-free workers." Established April 1999. Circulation: 15,000 unique visitors per month. Pays on acceptance. Byline given. Buys all rights. "Our response time to queries varies greatly from proposal to proposal. Impossible to give average time. If we like a proposal, we're likely to get back to the writer faster than if we don't like it."

E-mail for queries: egershon@aquent.com.

Editorial Needs: Essays, how-to, humor, interview, opinion, personal experience, technology, trade. Query with published clips. Word length for articles: generally between 750 and 2000.

Payment: $500–$1000. Payment for unsolicited articles varies, depends entirely upon specifics of article. Sometimes pays the expenses of writers on assignment.

Photos/Art: "We rarely use photos. No policy."

Advice from Market: "We post exhaustive guidelines on our site at http://www.aquent.com/sitemetatext/WritersGuidelines/Writers GuidelinesTofC.html."

Armchair Millionaire, http://armchairmillionaire.com
iVillage: The Women's Network, 170 Fifth Avenue, New York, NY 10010. Fax: (212) 604-9133. Kellie Krumplitsch, editorial director.

This market describes itself as "a community of people just like you—people who want to become financially independent without budgeting all the fun out of our lives. Our goal is to help [readers] build a million-dollar portfolio." The content includes columns on The Five Steps to Financial Freedom, The Model Portfolio, Savvy Investing, Fund-amentals, and other helpful how-to's targeting that first million dollars.

E-mail for queries: Kellie Krumplitsch at kellie@mail.ivillage.com.

[For full listing see Parent Soup on page 157.]

Atlanta CitySearch, http://www.atlanta.citysearch.com
Ticketmaster Online CitySearch, 790 East Colorado Blvd., Suite 200, Pasadena, CA 91101. Tel.: (626) 405-0050, fax: (626) 405-9929. Michael Phillips, editor.

"Even though we have multiple publications, most of the freelance sourcing is still done from our home office in Pasadena, CA. The process for someone submitting work to lasvegas.citysearch.com or austin.citysearch.com would be the same." (See "Advice from Market" below.) Twenty percent freelance written. "Ticketmaster Online City-Search is a leading provider of local city guides, local advertising, and live event ticketing on the Internet. The CitySearch city guides provide up-to-date information regarding arts and entertainment events, community activities, recreation, business, shopping, professional services and news/sports/weather to consumers in metropolitan areas. Ticketmaster Online offers consumers up-to-date information on live entertainment events and a convenient means of purchasing tickets for live events and related merchandise on the World Wide Web in 42 states and in Canada and the United Kingdom. Established September 1995. Circulation: withheld. Pays on acceptance. Byline given.

E-mail for queries: content_jobs@citysearch.com

Editorial Needs: Entertainment, music, travel, food. Query with published clips.

Payment: Varies.

Advice from Market: "The most common type of freelance work at CitySearch is made up of the 150-word descriptions of local restaurants, venues, tourist attractions, etc., which we use to build the base of our city guide sites. If a writer is interested in working with CitySearch, he or she should check our home page (www.citysearch.com) to see if the city which interests them has been launched. Look for "coming soon" and for other major cities that don't yet have CitySearch publications. If the city has not been launched, the writer should send clips, areas of expertise (music, food, tourism and travel, shopping, sports) to content_jobs@citysearch.com. Once the site is launched, the greatest need for freelancers is for food and shopping writers. They should follow the same directions as above."

Advice from Writers: "The best approach is to try to get to know the editor who deals with the area(s) you're interested in and start a dialogue with them. They seem to be at least somewhat open to negotiation re: money."

Atnewyork: The Silicon Alley Network, http://www.atnewyork.com Internet.com, 55 Broad Street, Suite 23F, New York, NY 10004. Tel.: (212) 425-8201, fax: (212) 425-8291. Tom Watson, founder and co-managing editor.

Less than 5 percent freelance written. @NY "covers New York's Silicon Alley high-tech business community." Established September

1995. Circulation: 100,000 unique visits per month. Pays on publication. Byline given. Buys online rights, exclusive. Reports in 2 weeks on queries.

E-mail for queries only (no submissions): twatson@internet.com.

Editorial Needs: Technology. Query with published clips. Word length for articles: 400–800.

Payment: $50–$200. Sometimes pays the expenses of writers on assignment.

Photos/Art: State availability of photos with submission. No additional payment.

Advice from Market: We occasionally use freelancers to cover events or to write profiles of up-and-coming companies.

At the Fence: Relationships and Parenting, http://www.atthefence.com At the Fence, 6002 Whippoorwill Rd., Tampa, FL 33625. Fax: (813) 969-1730. Nora Penia, editor.

"At the Fence is an online publication focusing on relationship issues of all kinds. Visitors read articles and letters and submit their own questions for an online answer. Readers range in age from teenagers to elderly, with a large percentage in the 25 to 45 range. Established December 1996. Circulation: 2000. Pays on publication. Byline given. Buys online publication rights, including remaining online indefinitely in archives. Accepts simultaneous and previously published submissions. Reports in 1–2 days on queries, 1–2 weeks on manuscripts. Ninety percent freelance written.

E-mail for submissions: editor@atthefence.com.

Editorial Needs: Essays, humor, inspirational, opinion, personal experience, religious, teen, women's, nonfiction articles relating to relationship issues and solutions to problems. Query or complete manuscript. Word length for articles: 500–2000.

Advice from Market: Writers may query a particular article or simply send it in the body of an e-mail to: editor@atthefence.com. Articles should have some connection to relationship issues and present useful information, solutions, encouragements, or humor. A wide range of topics will be considered appropriate; however, erotic material is not welcome. See www.atthefence.com/guidelines.htm.

Austin CitySearch, http://www.austin.citysearch.com
Ticketmaster Online CitySearch, 790 East Colorado Boulevard, Suite 200, Pasadena, CA 91101. Tel.: (626) 405-0050, fax: (626) 405-9929. Austin Office Tel.: (512) 472-1515. Michael Phillips, editor.

[For full listing see Atlanta CitySearch on page 97.]

Awe-Struck, www.awe-struck.net
Awe-Struck E-Books. Dick Claassen/Kathryn Struck, co-editors.

"We publish novels in electronic format: downloads and disks in the mail (Flopp-ebooks), novel-length (primarily) manuscripts in the romance and sci-fi genres and subgenres (sci-fi romance, romantic suspense, Native American fiction/romance); we also consider works of general fiction, and have a series of books called the Ennoble Series. All of the novels in the Ennoble series have central character(s) who are disabled. They are primarily romance novels and sci-fi novels, too. Mostly we like a good book! Not considering children's or poetry at this time." Established December 1998. Circulation: 1000. Byline given. Buys electronic rights only—international. Accepts simultaneous and previously published submissions. Reports in 2 weeks on queries, 1–2 months on manuscripts. "We close down new submissions if it gets much longer than that."

E-mail for queries: kathrynd@mwci.net.

Editorial Needs: Fiction. Query. Word length for books: "We like 70,000 words minimum on novels."

Payment: Royalties—40 percent of unit price less one half the credit-card server's "cut" (15 percent at this time). Complete contract is on site for perusal.

Advice from Market: "A query letter is necessary, with a synopsis and the first two chapters of the novel. Be sure to label the files with last name, and include the e-mail address at the beginning of the manuscript. We like RTF format [Rich Text Format; one of your "Save As" options]. Complete submission guidelines are on the Authors Submissions page (with a sample contract) on our site. Check the main menu for that link. Many writers try to send excerpts in antiquated programs that cannot be easily translated into the Word 97 program we use. We cannot do a heavy format on a novel. We already format for Nuvomedia (HTML), for Peanut Press and Librius (both use RTF). We use PDF for our own downloads. Basic formatting must be done by the author to be considered. Sometimes authors expect expensive-looking cover work for free. Covers sell books. We feature an artist (very good one!) who does covers for $300. We think that is a bargain. We can do text-only covers for no charge. Authors need to realize that it takes time, energy, and, unfortunately, money to get a book up and running. We are a small company that prides itself on personal contact, open communication, and author-publisher collabo-ration. We work hard for our clients. But we cannot afford (yet) some of the services that the bigger publishers may offer. We also like to see a new slant on old themes. We don't want to publish run-of-the-mill anything. Put a new twist on it. Add some humor. Don't develop stories that are reruns of other stories. Hold your nose and jump off the edge."

Bay Area CitySearch, http://www.bayarea.citysearch.com
Ticketmaster Online CitySearch, 790 East Colorado Blvd., Suite 200, Pasadena, CA 91101. Tel.: (626) 405-0050, fax: (626) 405-9929. Michael Phillips, editor.

[For full listing see Atlanta CitySearch on page 97.]

Best of the Web Anthology, The, http://www.pulpeternity.com
Eternity Press, P.O. Box 930068, Norcross, GA 30003. Steve Algieri, senior editor and publisher.

One hundred percent freelance written. This market describes itself as a "year-end anthology of the year's best Web-published fiction with an eye toward genre themes." Established September 1998. Circu-lation: 5000. Pays on publication of accompanying print anthology. Byline given. Buys onetime nonexclusive rights with one nonexclu-sive onetime anthology option. Accepts simultaneous and previously published submissions. Reports in 1 week on queries, 90 days on manuscripts.

E-mail for submissions: pulpeternity@hotmail.com.
Editorial Needs: Fiction, poetry. Send complete manuscript. Word length for stories: 40,000 maximum.
Payment: $10–$50.
Advice from Market: Stories must have been published in an online

serial publication or electronic newsletter (must have ISSN number) for the first time during that year. Prior print publication is allowed, previous year's electronic publication is not. Stories on personal Web sites, online unregistered e-zines and newsletters, or in newsgroups are not eligible. Queries regarding eligibility are accepted at the editorial address.

Bible Advocate Online, http://www.baonline.org.
General Conference of the Church Of God (Seventh Day), P.O. Box 33677, Denver, CO 80233. Tel.: (303) 452-7973, fax: (303) 452-0657. Calvin Burrell, editor.

Twenty-five to one hundred percent freelance written. This market describes itself as "a Christian magazine featuring articles on current social and religious issues, struggles of everyday life, Bible topics, and personal experience stories. We try to gear our material to the unchurched." Established October 1996. Circulation: withheld. Pays on publication. Byline given. Buys first, reprint, simultaneous rights. Accepts simultaneous and previously published submissions. Reports in 4–6 weeks on queries, 4–8 weeks on manuscripts.

E-mail for submissions: cofgsd@denver.net

Editorial Needs: Inspirational, personal experience, religious. Send complete manuscript. Word length for articles: 700–1500.

Payment: Around $50 for assigned articles (we don't assign many articles); $10–$35 for unsolicited articles.

Photos/Art: Send photos with submission. Negotiates payment individually. Captions required. Buys onetime rights.

Advice from Market: "You can download our guidelines and theme list at www.baonline.org. We look for articles that address the felt needs of the Internet audience (see our archives for examples). We prefer a contemporary writing style and an ability to explain the truths of the Bible and Christian life in terms an unchurched person can understand. Please watch your jargon!"

BiblioBytes, http://www.bb.com
This book's senior contributing writer Mark Palmer says "BiblioBytes claims to offer the 'best and most complete selection of electronic books available on the Internet,' which can be 'read instantly—right

now—without waiting for shipping or credit card processing. Any time. Any place.' BiblioBytes touts itself primarily as a place to read books for free; those seeking to submit for money should first consult the writer's contract at www.bb.com/contract.cfm." Peruse the site and query before submitting.

E-mail for queries: comment@bb.com.

Biztravel.com, http://www.biztravel.com
Biztravel.com, Inc., 220 East 23rd St., Suite 900, New York, NY 10010. Tel.: (212) 696-9800. Lauren Janis, senior editor.

Billed as "the Internet company for frequent business travelers," Biztravel.com provides tools for arranging seamless travel. They also offer editorial advice on issues that have to do with making your trip more bearable. Features include topics on how to deal with jet lag and where to look for your lost baggage. Lauren says Biztravel is "undergoing a transition," so be sure to peruse the site and query before submitting.

E-mail for queries: Lauren Janis at LJanis@biztravel.com.

Advice from Writers: ASJA's "Contracts Watch" reports that Biztravel.com "peddled a freelancer's piece to another Web site after its sublicensing right under contract had expired. The writer asked and collected triple the original fee." In that same issue of ASJA's "Contract Watch," a writer reported that "Biztravel.com limits online archive use to a year and readily agreed, on request, to add a royalty for other kinds of electronic use." Writers from NWU's database consistently reported payments of 50 cents/word and agreed that Biztravel.com "will not negotiate." However, while one writer reported parting with "all rights" with "no additional compensation," another writer was able to sell only "Web rights." Even with most rights secured, that freelancer still didn't think highly of writing for Biztravel.com, describing the experience as "poor pay, poor treatment, poor editing." [Please note that these writers' comments did not refer to this listing's contact, senior editor Lauren Janis.]

Blue Review, The, http://paulie.com/blue/guide.html
3420 N. Kachina Lane, Scottsdale, AZ 85281. Richard Russell, editor.

E-mail for queries: Richard Russell at rickrussell@paulie.com

Payment: "I pay five dollars per published piece. And, sometimes, when I see one of my artists needs money, [I] buy in advance."

Advice from Market: "The Blue Review publishes things that are different. Successful writers here are artists and approach the language as a large box of colors. There are no rules, except to write something in a way no one else ever has before. Literature will change over the next fifty years, as painting did a little over a century ago. The Blue Review seeks, more than anything else, to be the gallery for the literary Gauguins and Van Goghs that may get the recognition they deserve long after they can enjoy it."

Boston.com, http://www.boston.com
The Boston Globe. Tel.: (617) 929-2000 (they will forward you to Boston.com's office). Theresa Hanafin, online editor.

Boston.com is the NYTimes.com of Boston. Columns and features run the gamut, from national and international news to local arts and sports. Peruse the site and query before submitting.

E-mail for queries: Theresa Hanafin at Hanafin@boston.com.

Boston Sidewalk, http://www.boston.sidewalk.com
Microsoft, 54 Canal St., Suite 600, Boston MA 02114. Tel.: (617) 263-6000, fax: (617) 263-6073. Janice Page, executive producer.

"Guide to arts, entertainment, and shopping in Boston." Peruse the site and query before submitting.

E-mail for queries: Janice Page at jpage@microsoft.com.

[For full listing see New York Sidewalk listing on page 78.]

Brainplay.com, http://www.brainplay.com
Lisa Price, editor.

This book's senior contributing writer Karen Morrissey explains, "Brainplay.com is a market with 'the most comprehensive and in-depth information on kids' products available anywhere, on or off the Internet.' " This market didn't complete our questionnaire, but writers report that it pays for online freelance material. Peruse the site and query before submitting.

E-mail for queries: Lisa Price at lisaprice@brainplay.com.

Advice from Writers: "BrainPlay publishes parenting articles

(750 words) in trimesters. They pay $300 per article, and the piece goes online about three weeks after deadline date. They're great to work with."

Bridges.com, http://www.bridges.com
Bridges.com "specializes in continuous and customized publishing on the Internet," with their primary focus being "on services and products for the career development industry." Basically, they develop software to automate and customize content for companies and individuals. This market didn't complete our questionnaire but was very receptive to being including in this book. Peruse the site and send a query before submitting.
 E-mail for queries: smcmullan@bridges.com.

Business Week Online, http://www.businessweek.com
Julia Lichtblau, managing editor.
 The site is like its print counterpart, in that it specializes in all things business. Though this market didn't complete our questionnaire, Julia Lichtblau did confirm that Business Week Online "does use freelancers—including outside columnists—regularly. The amount waxes and wanes." Peruse the site and query before submitting.
 E-mail for queries: Julia Lichtblau at julia_lichtblau@business week.com.
 Advice from Writers: One writer describes Business Week Online as "a nightmare" based on the following experience. "I was given an assignment with a tight deadline. I got it in on time, only to wait weeks with no word from the editor. She finally sent a quick e-mail telling me that she wasn't sure if she had just a few questions, needed a rewrite, or would kill the story. Obviously she must not have read the story. Several weeks later, I contacted her again. She apologized profusely and promised to get back to me in a week or two. Two months later and still no word. We're not talking about a query here—we're talking about an actual assignment. For the 800- to 1200-word article I was to be paid $600. Not bad, but not great—and certainly not worth all the aggravation." [Please note that this writer's comments did not refer to this listing's contact, managing editor Julia Lichtblau.]

Cable World, http://www.cableworld.com
Intertec Publishing, 11 River Bend Dr. South, Stamford, CT 06907. Tel.: (203) 358-9900, fax: (203) 358-5823. Matt Stump, editor.

Cable World covers the cable industry, focusing on business news and noteworthy visionaries. Stories range from "FCC's Position on Open Access Questioned" to "AOL–TV Guide Ink Cyberspace Deal" and "Lee Masters Bets on Interactive Platform."

E-mail for queries: Matt_Stump@intertec.com.

[For full listing see Catalog Age below.]

Calendar Live!, http://www.calendarlive.com
John Forgetta, editor.

Calendar Live! is a CitySearch affiliate published and polished by the *L.A. Times* crew, covering all the goodies of regional guides—arts, entertainment, music, movies, travel, and all the facets of finding fun in the Los Angeles area.

This market didn't complete our questionnaire, but writers report that it pays for online freelance material. Peruse the site and query before submitting.

E-mail for resumes and clips only: John.Forgetta@latimes.com.

Advice from Market: "Calendarlive.com, while paying for original content, does not accept unsolicited manuscripts of any sort. Contributors are screened through an interview and writing process before freelance assignments are distributed."

Catalog Age, http://www.CatalogAgemag.com
Intertec Publishing, 11 River Bend Dr. South, Stamford, CT 06907. Tel.: (203) 358-9900, fax: (203) 358-5823. Laura Beaudry, editorial director.

Ten to twenty percent freelance written. Catalog Age says it "serves top executives in the mail order and electronic catalog markets. Readers are presidents, owners, CEOs, general managers, vice presidents." Established 1983. Circulation: withheld. Byline given. Buys worldwide exclusive publication rights for 60 days from first publication, reprint rights, rights to reproduce in other media. Sometimes pays the expenses of writers on assignment. Query.

E-mail for queries: Laura_Beaudry@intertec.com

Editorial Needs: how-to, technical, technology, company case studies, trends, news stories. Word length for articles: 600–2500.

Payment: Varies from $300–$2,000. Pays on acceptance.

Photos/Art: Send photos with submission. Negotiates payment individually. Requires identification of subjects. Buys all rights.

CDNOW, http://www.cdnow.com

CDNOW, 55 Broad St., 10th floor, New York, NY 10004. Tel.: (212) 378-5555, fax: (212) 742-1755. John Bitzer, editorial director.

Fifty percent freelance written. CDNOW describes itself as "interviews, features, and album reviews for all genres." Established 1994. Circulation: 1.7 million unique visits per month. Sometimes pays the expenses of writers on assignment. Byline given. Query with published clips.

E-mail for queries: jbitzer@cdnow.com

Editorial Needs: Music. Word length for articles: 150–1000.

Payment: Varies from $30 per album review to $400 for interviews. Pays on acceptance.

Advice from Market: "Prospective writers should always be familiar with the site—far too many just approach us blindly without knowing what we cover, or how we present it. Also, opportunities are more likely to exist in less popular—or more niche-oriented—genres."

Charged: Extreme Leisure, http://www.charged.com

Zap Internet Corp., 1700 Broadway, 9th floor, New York, NY 10019. Tel.: (212) 765-5239, fax: (212) 765-5933. Alice Bradley, editor in chief.

Seventy percent freelance written. "Charged is fetishes, blimps, crop circles, DJ'ing, swimmin' naked, singing, swinging, watching, making, doing, and everything in between. If you want to know what extreme leisure is, you have to read Charged. Our audience is made up mostly of college students and the disenfranchised post-college kids, as well as a smattering of fun-loving 30-year-olds with senses of humor." Originally established in April 1996 (closed March 1998); reopened May 1998. Circulation: withheld. Pays on acceptance. Byline given. Buys 60-day exclusive rights plus nonexclusive rights to republish on continuing basis in any form or media. Accepts simultaneous. Reports in 1 month on queries, 2 months on manuscripts.

E-mail for queries: edit@charged.com.

Editorial Needs: Book excerpts, entertainment, essays, health/ fitness, how-to, humor, fiction, general interest, interview, opinion, personal experience, travel, sports. Query with published clips. Word length for articles: 250–5000.

Payment: assigned articles, $250–$800; unsolicited articles, $150–$500. Sometimes pays the expenses of writers on assignment.

Photos/Art: State availability of photos with submission. Negotiates payment individually. Requires identification of subjects. Buys same rights as content rights, above.

Advice from Market: "The most frustrating thing for me is receiving queries or manuscripts from writers who have clearly never read Charged. I want our writers to not only read us, but also love us. Or at least like us a lot. Submissions with spelling mistakes will be judged harshly. We're tired of the 'Here I am, a newcomer to this sport/ activity/sex act, come to see what it's all about at this festival/conven- tion/sex club.' Show us something new. Humor is very, very important to us."

Charlotte CitySearch, www.charlotte.citysearch.com
Ticketmaster Online CitySearch, 790 East Colorado Blvd., Suite 200, Pasadena, CA 91101. Tel.: (626) 405-0050, fax: (626) 405-9929. Michael Phillips, editor.

E-mail for queries: content_jobs@citysearch.com

[For full listing see Atlanta CitySearch on page 97.]

Chartattack.com, http://www.chartattack.com
Chart Communications Inc., #200–41 Britain St., Toronto, Ontario M5A 1R7, Canada. Tel.: (416) 363-3101, fax: (416) 363-3109. Howard Druckman, music editor.

Ninety percent freelance written. This market describes itself as "news and features on Canadian and international music and pop culture scenes with an emphasis on the cutting edge. Readership: media-savvy youth market 15–30." Established March 1996. Circu- lation: 50,000 unique visits per month. Pays on acceptance. Byline given.

E-mail for queries: chart@chartnet.com.

Editorial Needs: Book excerpts, entertainment, music, teen. Query with published clips.

Payment: Varies from $10 for some reviews to $300 for a feature article.

Photos/Art: Send photos with submission. Negotiates payment individually.

Advice from Market: "Generally, we don't accept unsolicited material. We do work with writers in coming up with story ideas but mainly stories are assigned directly from our editorial office. Rarely do we publish unsolicited, completed stories. Keep in mind that our demographic is young and the music and pop culture (film, books, etc.) angle we take is one that is fairly edgy, appealing to a media- and consumer-savvy group."

Chicago Sidewalk, http://www.chicago.sidewalk.com
Microsoft, 440 N. Wells, Suite 320, Chicago, IL 60610. Tel.: (312) 396-8100, fax: (312) 396-1916. Steve Cvengros, executive producer.

"Guide to arts, entertainment, and shopping in Chicago." Peruse the site and query before submitting.

E-mail for queries: Steve Cvengros at stevecv@microsoft.com.

[For full listing see New York Sidewalk listing on page 78.]

Circulation Management, http://www.circman.com
Intertec Publishing, 11 River Bend Dr. South, Stamford, CT 06907. Tel.: (203) 358-9900, fax: (203) 358-5823. Karlene Lukovitz, editor.

Circulation Management covers just that, the circulation management industry—business-to-business, consumer marketing, agencies. CM readers peruse general news briefs as well as columns such as CM Idea Bank, Supplier News, and People.

E-mail for queries: karlene_lukovitz@intertec.com.

[For full listing see Catalog Age on page 106.]

Clean Sheets Erotica Magazine, http://www.cleansheets.com.
Clean Sheets Erotica Magazine, 3844 High St., Oakland, CA 94619. Mary Anne Mohanraj, editor in chief.

Fiction and poetry are 100 percent freelance written, nonfiction is about 50 percent. This market describes itself as an "Internet publication featuring intelligent and sexy erotic fiction, poetry, and art, as well as information and commentary on sexuality and society. Adult audience." Established October 1998. Circulation: 50,000. Pays on publication. Byline given. Buys onetime electronic publication rights; archival rights are separately negotiated and are nonexclusive. Accepts simultaneous and previously published submissions (if disclosed). Reports in 2 weeks on queries, 3 months on manuscripts.

E-mail for submissions: editor@cleansheets.com; fiction submissions: fiction@cleansheets.com; poetry submissions: poetry@cleansheets.com.

Editorial Needs: Book excerpts, erotica, fiction, poetry. Send complete manuscript. Word length for articles: fiction prefer 1000–5000; poetry prefer fewer than 100 lines.

Payment: Fiction 3 cents/word to 5000, 2 cents/word thereafter; poetry $10 first accepted, $20 thereafter. Lower rates for reprints.

Advice from Market: See submission guidelines at www.clean sheets.com.

ClubHaven: ClubCorp's exclusive online club,
http://www.clubhaven.com
ClubCorp USA, 3030 LBJ Freeway, Suite 350, Dallas, TX 75234. Tel.: (972) 888-7787, fax: (972) 888-7388. Lori Stacy, editor in chief.

"ClubHaven.com is a Web site for the Members and Guests of ClubCorp's over 200 country clubs, city clubs, resorts, daily-use golf facilities and city athletic clubs. We focus on the lifestyle interests of our nearly half-million members and cover subjects such as golf, tennis, fitness, nutrition, wine, cooking, cigars, books, finance, business, and the arts. One goal of the site is to encourage and build community among our members, either via their actual contributions, interviews with them as sidebars to articles, or articles that encourage feedback and discussion. We are also interested in promoting our clubs via articles about the clubs or the Employee Partners of these clubs, including chefs, fitness and golf pros, catering specialists, and meeting planner specialists." Established September 1998. Ninety percent freelance written. Circulation: 25,000. Pays on acceptance. Byline given. Buys all rights. Reports in 3 months on queries. "Please, no unsolicited manuscripts."

E-mail for queries: clubhaven@clubcorp.com.

Editorial Needs: Book excerpts, health/fitness, travel, sports, food, wine, cigars, business. Query with published clips. Word length for articles: 400–1500.

Payment: 50 cents per word. Pays the expenses of writers on assignment.

Advice from Market: "Writers should keep the medium in mind when submitting story ideas: what works in print does not always translate well into the interactive medium. When possible, stories should include interactive features such as links, and length should be no more than 1500 words per story (unless the story is presented in multiple sections)."

Advice from Writers: One freelancer describes ClubHaven as "inconsistent," explaining that "some writers get a time-limited license. Others get a work-for-hire."

CNET, http://www.cnet.com
Chris Barr, editor in chief.

CNET's tag line is "The source for computers and technology" and that's just what they are—a tech hub with tech information and links to techie things. They also provide editorial links to tech news." Topics include reviews of up-to-date software releases and hardware upgrades. CNET also covers gaming reviews and anything that is technology related—both domestic and international. Articles range from Web building products and consumer electronics to information on investing in new media stocks and finding technology jobs. Peruse the site and query before submitting.

E-mail for queries: Alice Hill at aliceh@cnet.com.

CNN.com, http://www.cnn.com
CNN Interactive is, yes, the interactive online service operated by Cable News Network, aka CNN. Basically, it's all things news. National and global. Freelance writing–wise, CNN's sites are quite guarded, right down to their receptionists at (404) 827-1500. But we were told that all queries for online sites could be sent to: Interactive Producer, Assignment Desk, CNN.com [or whichever of its sites you're querying], One CNN Center, P.O. Box 105366, Atlanta, GA 30348. One of our book's prerequisites was the acceptance of electronic queries, but

CNN's sites still qualify. They just prefer to whittle their queries via mail before electronic correspondence.

Advice from Writers: One online writer reported getting paid $1 a word for CNN's financial news site, CNNfn.com. A writer from NWU's database who got paid $1000 for first Web rights on CNN's CNNfn .com reported working with "a good editor but [who was] unclear on assignments" and recommended "getting the brief clearly upfront." Peruse the site and query before submitting.

CNNfn.com, http://www.cnnfn.com
This is the financial network Web site of CNN Interactive. Thorough like its parent Web site, CNN.com, CNNfn covers all things financial in the news, 24 hours a day, seven days a week. Think money and think information about it. Topics include personal investing in technology stocks as well as general financial news and happenings. The market tends to dictate the content, so keep ahead of the curve and watch for global trends. Peruse the site and query before submitting.

[For full listing see CNN.com on page 111.]

CNN Headline News, http://www.cnn.com/quicknews
This market bills itself simply as "24-Hour Non-Stop Headlines" and it's not kidding. Except for that funny part about being just headlines. It's a little more, but not much. Articles vary depending on the latest big thing; whether it be a hurricane off the coast of Florida or a revolution in the Balkans. It's news that warrants headline attention. Peruse the site and query before submitting.

[For full listing see CNN.com on page 111.]

CNN/Sports Illustrated, http://www.cnnsi.com
Sports plus news equals sporting news. Lots of it. They cover sports both nationally and internationally. This includes a range of topics in all sizes from college and pro to Little League and the century's all-time best. They are interactive which means they have articles that contain audio and/or video where appropriate. As expected, the content is, for the most part, dictated by the season.

[For full listing see CNN.com on page 111]

Collective, The, http://www.pulpeternity.com/thecollective
Eternity Press, P.O. Box 930068, Norcross, GA 30003. Steve Algieri, senior editor and publisher.

One hundred percent freelance written. This market describes itself as science fiction, fantasy, and horror. Established April 1999. Circulation: 5000. Pays on publication. Byline given. Buys first worldwide electronic rights with nonexclusive onetime anthology rights. Accepts simultaneous and previously published submissions. Reports in 1 week on queries, 90 days on manuscripts.

E-mail for submissions: collectivemag@hotmail.com.

Editorial Needs: Fiction. Send complete manuscript. Word length for stories: up to 3500.

Payment: 3 cents per word.

Advice from Market: The Collective is an online cooperative organization consisting of small press writers, editors, and publishers interested in working together to keep genre fiction alive. Membership is free, and we accept member submissions *only.* You must have a valid e-mail address to join. Our monthly e-mail newsletter features member fiction, writing articles, and industry news for editors, writers, and readers. Visit the Web site for more details.

Cyber Age Adventures, The: Weekly magazine of superhero fiction, http://www.cyberageadventures.com
Enduring Myth Productions, 432 South B St., Lake Worth, FL 33460. Tel.: (561) 540-5499, fax: (561) 588-7074. Frank Fradella, editor.

Eighty percent freelance written. "We provide excellent weekly superhero fiction to both comic book readers and those who may have outgrown that medium but still love superhero stories. Established January 1999. Circulation: 550. Pays on publication. Byline given. Buys onetime electronic rights. Accepts simultaneous and previously published submissions. Reports in 2 days maximum on queries, 2 weeks on manuscripts.

E-mail for submissions: CyberAge@iname.com.

Editorial Needs: Fiction. Send complete manuscript. Word length for stories: 3000 (for complete manuscript or part thereof in case of serials).

Payment: Flat rate of $20 per story, or part thereof in case of serials.

Photos/Art: State availability of photos with submission. No additional payment. Requirements: captions, model releases. identification of subjects. Buys onetime rights.

Advice from Market: "Our complete submission guidelines can be found on our Web site at http://www.cyberageadventures.com. The most common error that we see in writers' submissions is not following these guidelines closely enough. Beyond that, we *strongly* recommend that you actually read our magazine before submitting. Cyber Age Adventures is not just a comic book without the art. We work exclusively in prose because we are targeting a different audience. The comic book readers of the past are the book readers of today. Their tastes have matured, no longer being satisfied with the gimmicks or false deaths of yesteryear. We want great stories that make us care about the characters. Make us salivate to see them appear again. But please . . . whatever you do . . . do not send us a story where the hero beats up some thugs in an alley. It's been done to death and we prize originality above all else. We are creating the *next* age of superheroes, after all."

Cyber Oasis, http://people.delphi.com/eide491/oasis.html
David Eide, editor.

Sixty percent freelance written. This market describes itself as a "literary and writing resource pub for writers and readers of lively writing." Established January 1998. Circulation: 3000. Pays on publication. Byline given. Buys onetime or reprint rights. Editorial lead time 3 months. Accepts previously published submissions. Reports immediately on queries, 2–6 weeks on manuscripts.

E-mail for editorial submissions: eide491@earthlink.net.

Editorial Needs: Book excerpts, essays, fiction, interview, personal experience, poetry. Send complete manuscript. Word length for articles: 500–2500.

Payment: for assigned articles: $20–$50; unsolicited articles $10–$20.

Advice from Market: Keep to the idea of helping writers in the market and provide the best literary work one is capable of—tell your story in an engaging way.

CyberTip4theDay.com, http://www.CyberTip4theDay.com
P.O. Box 4489, Foster City, CA 94404. Dan Berman, editor.

One hundred percent freelance. "CyberTip4theDay.com offers 'tipletters' in a wide variety of (growing) categories to opt-in subscribers who visit the site and register for their free subscriptions." Pays on acceptance. Buys all rights. No reprints. Responds quickly. Sample at Web site. Subscription free (Web content is sponsor supported).

E-mail for more information and guidelines: editor@CyberTip.net.

Editorial Needs: "We have [many] categories (e.g., Auto, Beauty, Computer, Diet, ESL). We need writers to generate the daily tips for each category and also, in the near future, to serve as 'experts-in-residence' for the Web pages that will be associated with each category. This is an excellent 'ground-floor' opportunity for qualified writers, with expertise and interest in a particular subject area. Daily (tips are submitted for an entire month at one time). We are also amenable to opening new categories."

Payment: "The initial monthly compensation for generating 30 tips in a particular category is $300 per month. You get base pay and a share of ad revenue, as well as royalties on special reports, published electronically. Annual income potential is in the five-figure range (explained in our detailed guidelines). Interested writers should begin by requesting detailed info from editor@CyberTip.net. This will explain the process in detail. The URL for more information is: http://www.CyberTip4theDay.com/jobs.htm."

Advice from Market: "Query messages laden with misspellings and other errors don't create a good first impression. They reflect a lack of conscientiousness. In sum, what we are looking for falls in the category of "Web content." This is an excellent opportunity for qualified, top-notch writers, with interest and expertise in particular subject areas. (By the way, the entire site is PG-rated and family friendly.)"

Datecentral.com, http://www.datecentral.com
At press time for this book, this market was on temporary hiatus to complete their redesign. No contact information was available. But writers have been paid by them in the past for online freelance material. Peruse the site and send a query before submitting (to an e-mail

address that you'll have to get from perusing their forthcoming site; or check with this book's companion Web site, www.marketsforwriters .com, and we'll let you know if any information has become available.

DaveCentral, http://www.DaveCentral.com
Andover Advanced Technologies, 50 Nagog Park Rd., 2nd floor, Acton, MA 01720. Tel.: (978) 635-5300, fax: (978) 635-5326. Robin Miller, senior editor.

DaveCentral is a proud part of the AndoverNews Network whose primary function is software archiving. DaveCentral specializes in software reviews and tends to do a lot of legwork for readers in terms of figuring out what to use and what to steer clear of. It also provides pertinent downloads and upgrades.

[For full listing see AndoverNews on page 94.]

DBUSINESS.COM: Local business starts here,
http://www.dbusiness.com
American Digital Media, tel.: (954) 776-5279, fax: (954) 776-7932. Kurt Greenbaum, editor.

"We are writing about emerging growth companies in local markets for an online business news network, providing updated, real-time news and information to company executives, investors, and people who seek sales leads for their own companies. Our focus is on small- to mid-cap public companies and venture-backed private companies." Established 1997. "Fifty percent freelance written now, [though] that will be reduced as we hire more full-time staff."

Circulation: 300,000. Pays on publication. Byline given. Buys all publication rights.

E-mail for queries: editor@dbusiness.com.

Editorial Needs: "Generally, we seek freelancers who are available in the markets we're covering. If we require a freelancer in that market, it is usually because we need someone to write breaking news for a select period of the day. There may be a need for more 'feature-oriented' writing about local businesses, but that hasn't been established yet." Query with published clips. Word length for articles: 300–600.

Payment: "Varies based on the writing done, $35–$200." Pays the expenses of writers on assignment.

Denver CitySearch, http://www.denver.citysearch.com
Ticketmaster Online CitySearch, 790 East Colorado Blvd., Suite 200, Pasadena, CA 91101. Tel.: (626) 405-0050, fax: (626) 405-9929. Denver Office Tel.: (303) 458-7090. Michael Phillips, editor.
   E-mail for queries: content_jobs@citysearch.com.
   [For full listing see Atlanta CitySearch on page 97.]

Denver Sidewalk, http://www.denver.sidewalk.com
Microsoft, 1390 Lawrence St., #400, Denver, CO 80204. Tel.: (303) 454-6500, fax: (303) 454-6539. Joe Rassenfoss, executive producer.
   "Guide to arts, entertainment and shopping in Denver."
   E-mail for queries: Joe Rassenfoss at joerasse@microsoft.com.
   [For full listing see New York Sidewalk listing on page 78.]

Detroit CitySearch, http://www.detroit.citysearch.com
Ticketmaster Online CitySearch, 790 East Colorado Blvd., Suite 200, Pasadena, CA 91101. Tel.: (626) 405-0050, fax: (626) 405-9929. Michael Phillips, editor.
   E-mail for queries: content_jobs@citysearch.com.
   [For full listing see Atlanta CitySearch on page 97.]

Developer.com, http://www.developer.com
EarthWeb's Developer.com touts itself as "the leading resource for developers." Web developers, that is. The wealth of information provided includes news, training, calendar of developer events, and an "Ask the Experts" column. Topics range from choosing the best HTML editors to the latest beta releases. EarthWeb provides the following guidelines, applicable to its network of sites:
   Editorial Needs: Generally they assign either a "Tech Focus" (around 1000 words) or a "Tech Workshop" (around 700 words plus source code). A Tech Focus is a detailed look at a specific technology that does not necessarily include code or examples, whereas a Tech Workshop is a hands-on tutorial.
   Payment: "EarthWeb (this market's publisher) pays its writers competitive rates. Please contact us directly about payment."
   Advice from Market: "Thank you for your interest in writing for

EarthWeb! To assist you and to provide consistency in our content, we've prepared some basic style, tone, and format guidelines. Please always keep in mind that our core audience is developers and designers. They are sophisticated, highly technical people who work on a variety of platforms with a range of technologies and are therefore familiar with technical terms and concepts. Tone: Articles should be straightforward and concise, not chatty. Please don't inject a personal perspective. Style points: We use the serial comma. So it's 'developers, programmers, and designers.' It's 'Web site' not website or web site. Companies are treated as single entities. 'Sun released its new spec,' not 'their new spec.' Capitalize languages and abbreviations: Perl, CGI, HTML, Java, DOS. Spell out "%." Spell out numbers one through nine; for 10 and up use numerals. URLs, e-mail addresses, and file names are always lowercase: www.earthweb.com, earth.gif,jane @earthweb.com. Submission Instructions: 1. Please submit your article in ASCII text in the body of an e-mail message. Also attach a text file. 2. Any accompanying graphics should be attached in .gif format. 3. Provide contact info in case we have questions for you during the edit. 4. Please submit a brief (30 words or less) author's bio. 5. Send your invoice along with your article via e-mail. You should receive payment within 30 days of publication."

Direct, http://www.directmag.com
Intertec Publishing, 11 River Bend Dr. South, Stamford, CT 06907. Tel.: (203) 358-9900, fax: (203) 358-5823. Ray Schultz, editor.

Direct cites itself as "The Magazine of Direct Marketing Management." It offers links, news—"Direct newsline for your daily source of news that matters to the direct marketing industry"—features, and regular columns on direct marketing breakthroughs and movers and shakers.

E-mail for submissions: ray_schultz@intertec.com.

[For full listing see Catalog Age on page 106.]

Discovery Channel Online, http://www.discovery.com
Tel.: (301) 986-0444. Andrea Meditch, editorial director.

[See full listing on page 72 in "Top Ten Places to Be Published Online."]

Diskus Publishing, http://www.diskuspublishing.com
DiskUs Publishing, P.O. Box 43, Albany, IN 47320. Tel.: (765) 789-4064, fax: (765) 789-4993. Marilyn Nesbitt, senior editor.

One hundred percent freelance written. "We sell e-books as downloads and disks in the mail. We sell in a variety of formats, and we also have our books available for most of the dedicated e-readers like RocketEbook, Softbook, and for the Librius Millennium. We publish books in every genre except erotica." Established April 1998. Circulation: 5000. Byline given. "We only lease the copyright of your book for one year. After that if you decide not to renew your contract all rights revert back to you." Accepts simultaneous and previously published submissions. Reports in 4–6 weeks on queries, 4 months on manuscripts.

E-mail for submissions: submissions@diskuspublishing.com.

Editorial Needs: Fiction, general interest, historical, inspirational, religious, technical, technology, teen, sports. Send complete manuscript.

Payment: "We pay 40 percent royalties of the download price of each sale. Our downloads sell for $3.50 so the author makes $1.40 for each sale made from our site. Word length for articles: no minimum or maximum.

Photos/Art: "The only thing we use artists for is for the covers of our books and for illustrations in children's books. We either pay upfront on these or we pay royalties."

Advice from Market: See http://members.tripod.com/diskus_publishing/submission.htm.

E Business, http://www.hp.com/ebusiness
This book's senior contributing writer Mark Palmer explains, "Hewlett-Packard's E Business magazine is all that. Business, I mean. A brief perusal of this site, however, will lend a more colorful feel than the stoic impression one may (or may not) associate with the *Wall Street Journal* or perhaps the *Times*. If this genre of reading/writing is your forte, you may be interested in poking around their site. . . . a site with some well-worded business perspectives." Peruse the site and query before submitting.

E-mail for queries: megan-taylor@hp.com.

Advice from Writers: One writer from NWU's database reported selling "first electronic rights" for payments of "$500 for department stories (750 words) and $1000 for features." The writer stated: "I have not tried to negotiate the fee, but I did ask that all the rights revert to me 30 days after initial publication. Editors OK'd that [without a] fuss. (Their contract states that E Business owns the rights but will grant permission to the writer to reprint the article in other places. I did grant E Business the right to leave the articles on its site (in the Back Issues section) indefinitely. Amy [managing editor Amy Cowen] is very responsive and pleasant, and concerned that her writers get paid on time. She's a good editor, too."

Editor & Publisher Interactive, http://www.mediainfo.com
The Editor & Publisher Co., 11 West 19th St., 10th floor, New York, NY 10011. Tel.: (212) 675-4380, fax: (212) 691-7287. Carl Sullivan, editor.

"E&P Interactive is the Web site for the online news industry and the newspaper industry (which mirrors our company's roots. E&P magazine has been serving the print newspaper industry for 115 years). Our mission is to cover all facets of the online news business: journalism, ethics, e-commerce, advertising, competition, etc." Established 1996. Seventy percent freelance written. Circulation: 100,000. Pays on publication. Byline given. Buys first-time, nonexclusive rights. Accepts simultaneous submissions. Reports in 1 week on queries; 3–4 weeks on manuscripts.

E-mail address for editorial submissions: editor@mediainfo.com.

Editorial Needs: Essays, how-to, interview, opinion, technology, trade. Query with published clips. Word length for articles: 200–no maximum.

Payment: $100–$300. Sometimes pays the expenses of writers on assignment.

Photos/Art: Send photos with submission. Negotiates payment individually. Requires captions and identification of subjects. Buys onetime rights.

Advice from Market: "My best advice is take a look at our site before submitting a query. Find out who we are and what we're interested in before sending ideas. Nothing is more annoying than a blind inquiry from a writer who hasn't done his/her homework on the publication in question."

EncycloZine, http://encyclozine.com
"EncycloZine is an encyclopedic e-zine with concise articles on a wide range of topics, and links to the best Web sites for further detailed study." Peruse the site and query before submitting.

Editorial Needs: "Currently looking for authors/encyclopedists who can write concise encyclopedia-style articles on a wide range of topics. At this time, we need broad surveys rather than in-depth articles, which will probably come later. Surveys should introduce significant topics at approximately a high-school level, and should be accompanied by a short list (e.g., 5 or so) of the very best sites for further study."

E-mail for queries: "Contact jenny@encyclozine.com for further details." (An alternative contact is Alan Richmond at alan@encyclozine.com.)

Epicurious, For People Who Eat, http://www.epicurious.com
CondéNet, 140 East 45th St., 37th floor, New York, NY 10017. (Note: CondéNet may be moving to 342 Madison Ave. Be sure to confirm address.) Gail Glickman Horwood, editor.

Ten percent freelance written. "Epicurious Food is about cooking and enjoying food—the Web destination for people who eat. It combines recipes and editorial from *Gourmet* and *Bon Appétit* magazines with Epicurious-generated features and interactivity, which together provide a comprehensive source for daily and special-occasion food information." Established September 1995. Circulation: 2 million. Pays on acceptance. Byline given. Buys all rights. Pieces are works made for hire.

E-mail for queries only: adwyer@condenet.com. ("We have never accepted an unsolicited submission.")

Editorial Needs: Articles on food.

Payment: "About $1 per word." Query with published clips. Word length for articles: 250–500. Sometimes pays the expenses of writers on assignment.

Photos/Art: Buys all rights.

E-scape: The Digital Journal of Speculative Fiction,
http://www.interink.com/escape.html
P.O. Box 165322, Kansas City, MO 64116. Allison Stein, editor.

"E-scape publishes science, fantasy, and horror fiction, and anything in between." One hundred percent freelance written. Peruse the site and query before submitting.

E-mail for queries: escape@interink.com; mail fiction submissions to above address.

Payment: 1 cent per word for fiction. Word length for stories: 500–5,000. "Does not pay for nonfiction."

ESPN.com, http://www.espn.com
Starwave Corporation, 13810 SE Eastgate Way, Bellevue, WA 98005. John Marvel, executive producer.

Formerly ESPN Sportszone, ESPN.com is still the total sports hub, consisting of current sporting news and editorial commentary with related partnerships with several other sporting venues/sites (e.g., NFL.com, NBA.com, WNBA.com, NASCAR, NHL.com, ABCSports, etc.). Peruse the site and query before submitting.

Phone number for queries: John Marvel at (425) 468-4000.

Eternity, The Online Journal of the Speculative Imagination,
http://www.pulpeternity.com
Eternity Press, P.O. Box 930068, Norcross, GA 30003. Steve Algieri, senior editor and publisher.

One hundred percent freelance written. This market describes itself as "genre fiction and poetry. Science fiction, fantasy, horror, suspense/thrillers, mysteries, historical, and fantastic romance all welcome." Established June 1997. Circulation: 5000. Pays on publication. Byline given. Buys first worldwide electronic rights with nonexclusive onetime anthology option at additional payment. Accepts simultaneous and previously published submissions. Reports in 1 week on queries, 60 days on manuscripts.

E-mail for submissions: pulpeternity@hotmail.com.

Editorial Needs: Fiction, poetry. Send complete manuscript. Word length for articles: up to 20,000.

Payment: Assigned articles, ¼ cent per word–½ cent per word; unsolicited articles, ¼ cent per word to $50; poetry, $2; bonus if selected to year-end print anthology.

Advice from Market: "Visit the site and read the magazine to see what we publish. Updated guidelines continually posted at www.pulp eternity.com/gl/index.htm. Sometimes do special projects and themed issues. Always include cover letter. Want edge fiction with characters my readers can empathize with. Look for ethnic, alternative sexuality, erotic, and feminist themes. Be yourself and write a story that matters."

Event Horizon: Science Fiction, Fantasy, and Horror, http://www.eventhorizon.com/sfzine
Event Horizon Web Productions, 48 Eighth Ave., Suite 405, New York, NY 10014. Tel.: (212) 989-3742. Ellen Datlow, editor.

This market describes itself as "literary sf/f/h fiction and nonfiction related to those genres plus weekly net interviews/chats with sf/f/h luminaries." Established August 1998. Ninety-eight percent freelance written. Circulation: 20,000. Pays on acceptance. Byline given. Buys first electronic rights and "others when can." Reports in a few weeks on nonfiction queries, 3 weeks on fiction on manuscripts.

E-mail address: Datlow@eventhorizon.com.

Editorial Needs: "No unsolicited fiction or nonfiction" [at the time this book went to press]. Word length for articles: 500–no maximum.

Payment: "Minimum 5 cents a word for fiction up to $250; $100 per column, $10–$25 per book review."

Advice from Market: "No unsolicited submissions [at the time this book went to press], but if an author has been professionally published he/she can query at Datlow@eventhorizon.com."

Family.com, http://www.family.com
Buena Vista Internet Group, 19 East 34th St., 6th floor, New York, NY 10016. Emily Smith, editor in chief.

"Family.com is an online resource aiming to help families have fun and raise great kids. It is written and designed principally for parents." Established 1996. Circulation: withheld. Ten percent freelance written. Pays on publication. Buys all rights.

E-mail for queries (no unsolicited submissions): editor_in_chief@ family.com.

Editorial Needs: Health/fitness, travel, parenting, education, food, baby/pregnancy. Query with published clips. Word length for articles: 500–2000.

Payment: Varies.

Advice from Market: "We are not currently looking for new free-lance writers. Our editorial needs are being met by our current roster. We will not send a 'thanks but no thanks' letter and it will be a rare exception if we respond at all."

Fashion Window, http://www.fashionwindow.com
At press time for this book, Fashion Window was poised for its relaunch. Karen W. Bressler says she's handling the editorial content and is always open to new ideas. Peruse the site and query before submitting.

E-mail for queries: Karen Bressler at karen@fashionwindow.com.

Advice from Market: "Writers should approach me with relevant topics on fashion related to style, TV, film, careers, etc. (see site for examples). . . . We will probably pay $400 for a 500-word article, which is typical length."

Fashion Windows, http://www.fashionwindows.com
[See full listing on page 74 in "Top Ten Places to be Published Online."]

Faulkner, http://www.faulkner.com
Tel.: (800) 843-0460.

This book's senior contributing writer Karen Morrissey explains, "Faulkner Information Services is a forum for 'unbiased, straight-forward intelligence about the technology enablers, products, services, and major players moving the marketplace.' " This market chose not to complete our questionnaire. Peruse the site and query before submitting.

E-mail for queries: Geoff Keston at editors@faulkner.com.

Feed, http://www.feedmag.com
[See full listing on page 77 in "Top Ten Places to be Published Online."]

15 Minutes, A Worthwhile Waste of Time, http://15minutes.com
15 Minutes Press. Benjamin Serrato, publisher.

This market describes itself as "pop culture commentary." One hundred percent freelance written. Established December 1995. Circulation: withheld. Pays on publication. Byline given sometimes. Buys all rights. Accepts simultaneous and previously published submissions.

E-mail for queries: Submissions@15minutes.com.

Editorial Needs: Humor, general interest. Send complete manuscript. Word length for articles: 100–1200.

Payment: $5–$50.

Fine Fishing, http://www.finefishing.com
Lou Bignami, editor and publisher.

This book's senior contributing writer Karen Morrissey explains, "Fine Fishing Internet Magazine embraces fishing in every sense of the sport, with over 30 articles per month covering saltwater and freshwater fishing, and fly-fishing." Peruse the site and query before submitting.

E-mail for queries: Lou Bignami at bignami@finefishing.com.

Fine Travel, http://www.finetravel.com
Lou Bignami, editor and publisher.

This book's senior contributing writer Karen Morrissey explains, "Fine Travel features 'over 200 articles from professional travel writers on mostly posh travel.' Content covers resorts and hotels, golf, skiing, cruises, fine dining and historical destinations." Peruse the site and query before submitting.

E-mail for queries: Lou Bignami at bignami@finetravel.com.

Fitness & Beauty Channel: IVillage, http://www.ivillage.com/fitness
iVillage: The Women's Network, 170 Fifth Ave., New York, NY 10010. Fax: (212) 604-9133. Kellie Krumplitsch, editorial director.

IVillage's fitness & beauty channel runs the complete spectrum of this comprehensive category—skin care, sports, shopping, dieting, and related dilemmas of the week. As usual, the emphasis is on helpful articles. Short how-to's to keep readers fit and feeling beautiful.

E-mail for queries: Clare Weiss at weiss@mail.ivillage.com.
[For full listing see Parent Soup on page 157.]

FitnessLink, All the News That's Fit, http://www.fitnesslink.com
FitnessLink, 113 Circle Dr. South, Lambertville, NJ 08530. Tel.: (609) 397-7664, fax: (609) 397-7347. Shannon Entin, editor.

Ninety percent freelance written. This market describes itself as "exercise, diet, nutrition, and workout information for the beginner to the athlete. Audience is about 60 percent women, 40 percent men, ages ranging from teens through seventies." Established March 1996. Circulation: 600,000. Pays on publication. Byline given. Buys first electronic rights. Accepts simultaneous and previously published submissions. Reports in 4–6 weeks on queries, 4–8 weeks on manuscripts.

E-mail for queries: editor@fitnesslink.com.

Editorial Needs: Health/fitness, men's, sports, women's. Query with published clips. Word length for articles: 200–1000.

Payment: $25–$150. Sometimes pays the expenses of writers on assignment.

Photos/Art: State availability of photos with submission. No additional payment.

Advice from Market: See www.fitnesslink.com/guide.htm.

Folio, http://www.foliomag.com
Intertec Publishing, 11 River Bend Dr. South, Stamford, CT 06907. Tel.: (203) 358-9900, fax: (203) 358-5823. Barbara Love, editor.

Folio bills itself as "The Magazine for Magazine Management," covering market forecasts, Q&A's, e-commerce, and editorial strategies, to name a few facets. Folio also keeps on top of industry news, software, issues and noteworthy contemporaries, with an overall view and appreciation of business aplomb.

E-mail for queries: barbara_love@intertec.com.
[For full listing see Catalog Age on page 106.]

Food Channel: IVillage, http://www.ivillage.com/food
iVillage: The Women's Network, 170 Fifth Ave., New York, NY 10010. Fax: (212) 604-9133. Kellie Krumplitsch, editorial director.

IVillage's food channel covers not just recipes, nutrition, baking, and cooking, but also shopping and saving preparation time, along with uniting the community of, well, everyone who eats. Most articles have that how-to feel, and seasonal eats would seem to be an ongoing opportunity for new how-to takes on every culinary category.

E-mail for queries: Jenny Saltiel at jsaltiel@mail.ivillage.com.

[For full listing see Parent Soup on page 157.]

G21: The World's Magazine, http://www.g21.net
Generator 21, 2916 N. Calvert St., #2A, Baltimore, MD, 21218. Tel.: (410) 889-4438, fax: same—call first. Rod Amis, editor and publisher.

Fifty percent freelance written. This market describes itself as a "weekly international magazine of news, humor, satire, and social commentary. We publish writers from four continents and have a strong interest in 'on the ground' international perspectives. We have been described in reviews as 'leftist.' " Established March 1996. Circulation: 50,000. Pays on publication. Byline given. Buys first publication only. Author retains all serial rights. Accepts simultaneous submissions. Reports in 1 week on queries, 1 week on manuscripts.

E-mail for queries: rod@g21.net.

Editorial Needs: Entertainment, essays, exposé, humor, general interest, historical, interview, music, opinion, personal experience, sports. ("We suggest that interested authors read our publication to see what types of material are appropriate.") Query. Word length for articles: 700–2000.

Payment: Assigned articles, $50–negotiable maximum; unsolicited articles, $50–$100.

Photos/Art: State availability of photos with submission. Negotiates payment individually. Requires model releases, identification of subjects. Buys onetime rights.

Advice from Market: "Again, we think it important the writers seeking to publish with the G21 read the Web magazine first. Our editorial position is extremely clear. Missing deadline is the supreme sin. We'll never consider anyone who misses a deadline again. We expect clearly written English, concision, and some degree of passion about the subject matter. We write for an international audience, so we expect stories/submissions of broad-based interest."

Gamelan.com, http://www.gamelan.com
EarthWeb's Gamelan is a Java-lovers heaven—Java programming source code, tutorials, news, community, a calendar of events, discussion groups, game development, business breakthroughs and uses, profiles, e-commerce applications, all around tech fun for Java prodigies or wannabes. For guidelines, see Developer.com, p. 117.

Gardenatprem.com, http://www.gardenatprem.com
PremDotCom, 501 Fifth Ave., Suite 2201, New York, NY 10017. Tel.: (212) 953-2539, fax: (212) 953-2525. M. Dahan, editor/chairman.

"Everything you need to know about your garden." Established September 1999. One hundred percent freelance written. Circulation: withheld. Pays on publication. Byline given sometimes. Buys "publication" rights.

E-mail for queries: Editor@prem.com.

Editorial Needs: Book excerpts, entertainment, exposé, health/fitness, how-to, humor, fiction, general interest, historical, inspirational, interview, men's, music, new product, opinion, personal experience, poetry, technical, technology, teen, travel, sports, women's. Query. Word length for articles: 300–no maximum.

Payment: $50–$1000. Sometimes pays the expenses of writers on assignment.

Photos/Art: State availability of photos with submission. Negotiates payment individually. Requires captions. Buys onetime rights.

Advice from Market: See section at http://www.prem.com on article submissions.

GenerationJ.com, http://www.generationj.com
Jewish Family & Life, 56 Kearney Rd., Needham, MA 02494. Tel.: (781) 449-9894, fax: (781) 449-9825. Ronnie Friedland, managing editor.

GenerationJ is a Web zine for "Generation X with a Jewish twist." Columns cover relationships, spirituality, lifestyles, health and fitness, social action, culture, and more—all with positive attitudes and community takes on general topics. Established October 1997. Eighty percent freelance written. Circulation: 100,000. Pays on acceptance. Byline given. Buys first publication rights—"exclusive rights for six months, then author can resell and author keeps profits—although

GenerationJ reserves the right to use in future anthologies." Accepts simultaneous and previously published submissions. Reports in 3 months on queries. "Don't want manuscripts."

E-mail address for queries: jflronnie@aol.com.

Editorial Needs: Jewish book excerpts, essays, health/fitness, interview, personal experience, travel, women's, Jewish parenting, Jewish spiritual. Query with published clips. Word length for articles: 400–800. "We put a Jewish spin on all content, be it health, book reviews, parenting issues, holiday celebrations."

Payment: $25 (for guest columns)–$200. Payment for unsolicited articles: $25–$100. Pays expenses of writers on assignment.

Photos/Art: Freelancers should send photos with submission. No additional payment.

Advice from Market: "Check our Web zines before querying—be sure you don't duplicate what we already have. . . . We put a Jewish values spin on everything. We are actively soliciting members of interfaith families to share their experiences."

GettingIt, http://www.gettingit.com
Allyson Quibell, managing editor.

GettingIt is a slick, savvy zine covering culture and consumption, music, celebrity dirt, soon-to-be trends, sex, scandal, tech toys, and first-person forays delivered with literary finesse. Although Allyson Quibell couldn't complete our questionnaire, she did stress that "we do indeed pay writers for content!" Peruse the site and query before submitting.

E-mail for queries: Allyson Quibell at aquibell@gettingit.com.

GFN.com: The Gay Financial Network, http://www.gfn.com
GFN.com, 111 Broadway, 12th floor, New York, NY 10006. Tel.: (212) 349-1659, fax: (212) 349-6100. Jeffrey L. Newman, executive editor.

"The leading online news site of financial and business news tailored to the gay and lesbian community." Established April 1998. Sixty percent freelance written. Circulation: 750,000. Pays on acceptance. Byline given. "Prefers [to buy] exclusive, but not necessary." Accepts simultaneous and previously published submissions.

E-mail for submissions: editor@gfn.com.

Editorial Needs: Book excerpts, entertainment, exposé, health/fitness, general interest, interview, men's, music, new product, personal experience, technical, technology, trade. Query. Word length for articles: 700–4000.

Payment: $75–$1000. Sometimes pays the expenses of writers on assignment.

Photos/Art: State availability of photos with submission. No additional payment.

Golf.com, http://www.golf.com
Patrick Jones, senior editor.

Writers report that Golf.com pays for online freelance material. Content includes commentary on tournaments and the players, equipment information, and some golfing instruction. Peruse the site and query before submitting.

E-mail for queries: Patrick Jones at patrick@golf.com.

Good Buys on the Net E-Zine, http://www.goodbuys.com
White Eagle Technologies, 2201 Greenvalley Dr., Carrollton, TX 75007. Tel.: (972) 446-1073.

A promotional e-zine with not merely promotional content. Past articles include "Hiding on the NET—A Must for Privacy" and "Show Your Friends How to Be Their Own Technical Support." This market hasn't completed our questionnaire, but one writer/publisher reported that it's a paying e-zine. Peruse the site, specifically the current e-zine issue, and query before submitting.

E-mail for queries: Bob Bell at sales@goodbuys.com.

GORP, The Great Outdoor Recreation Pages, http://www.gorp.com
GORP.com, 234 Berkeley Pl., Brooklyn, NY 11217. Tel.: (718) 638-9310, fax: (718) 857-3026. Eileen Gunn, managing editor.

Thirty-three percent freelance written. "GORP is committed to helping people pursue an active outdoors lifestyle. We publish articles on hiking, biking, paddling, fishing, camping, scenic driving, climbing, trekking, and other aspects of outdoor recreation and active travel." Established January 1995. Circulation: 1 million. Pays on publication. Byline given. Buys nonexclusive permanent electronic rights only. Accepts simultaneous and previously published submissions. Reports in 1–3 weeks on queries, 1 week to 2 months on manuscripts.

E-mail for queries: eileeng@gorp.com.

Editorial Needs: Active travel, as described above. Query, query with published clips, or send complete manuscript. [See page 22 for Eileen's favorite query and why it's her favorite.] Word length for articles: 1200–5000.

Payment: $100–$200 and up.

Photos/Art: State availability of photos with submission. Pays $10. Requires captions, identification of subjects. Buys nonexclusive permanent electronic rights.

Advice from Market: See http://www.gorp.com/gorp/freelance/ for the whole story.

Gowanus: An International Online Journal of Idea & Observation, http://www.dorsai.org/~tjhubsc/gowanus.html
473 17th St. #6, Brooklyn, NY 11215-6226. Tel.: (718) 965-3756 Fax: Same. Thomas J. Hubschman, publisher.

Seventy-five percent freelance written. "Gowanus is primarily a vehicle for writers in Third World countries. Emphasis is on the personal point of view, though all prose forms are welcome: essay, article, short story. Our readers are worldwide." Established June 1997. Circulation: in the thousands. Pays on publication. Byline given. Buys electronic publication and archiving, plus onetime print rights (such as in an anthology). Accepts simultaneous and previously published submissions (all assuming copyright is the author's). Reports in days on queries, weeks manuscripts.

E-mail for submissions: tjhubsc@dorsai.org.

Editorial Needs: Book excerpts, essays, fiction, general interest, interview, personal experience. Articles about politics and culture in the author's home country/region; reviews of books and indigenous periodicals. Query for nonfiction; send complete manuscript for fiction. Word length for articles: 1000–4000.

Payment: $15–$25.

Photos/Art: State availability of photos with submission. Negotiates payment individually. Requires identification of subjects. Buys same rights as on manuscripts.

Advice from Market: "As always, the best guidelines come from reading the publication itself. We deal with writers whose first language frequently is not English. If the submission is a good one and appropriate to the publication, we do in-depth work to help the author realize her or his idea/story. Most common mistake made by submitters: Sending inappropriate material because they have not actually read the publication but are attracted by the fact that we are a paying market." See http://www.dorsai.org/~tjhubsc/response.htm for more information.

GunGames Online: America's Favorite Shooting & Recreation Magazine, http://www.gungames.com
Millennium Publishing Group, P.O. Box 516, Moreno Valley, CA 92556. Tel.: (909) 485-7986, fax: (909) 485-6628. Michael Bane, editor.

"GunGames is the only newsstand publication in the USA that is exclusively focused on sports and recreation shooting. Its audience covers the 80 million Americans who own guns and use them primarily for sports and recreation shooting." Established October 1995. Fifty percent freelance written. Circulation: 250,000. Pays on publication. Byline given. Buys first North American rights. Accepts previously published submissions. "E-mail queries are answered within 48 hours."

E-mail for queries (no unsolicited manuscripts): michaelbane@ gungames.com.

Editorial Needs: Book excerpts, entertainment, essays, health/ fitness, how-to, humor, general interest, interview, men's, opinion, personal experience, technical, technology, teen, trade, travel, sports, women's. Query. "If we like the idea and are not familiar with the writer, we'll ask for clips." Word length for articles: "For Web articles, I like to see them in the 1000-word range; or even shorter, broken into sidebars."

Payment: $100.

Photos/Art: State availability of photos with submission. Negotiates payment individually. Requires captions, model releases, identification of subjects. Buys onetime rights.

Advice from Market: "It sends me screaming for freelancers to blind-query me or to send me some nitwit bogus 'angle'—I know your magazine is about wombats, but even wombats need good computing skills. We write about the sporting use of firearms; as a veteran editor (9 magazines as editor; one of the top magazine freelancers in the country; 19 books; featured in 2 journalism textbooks), I expect quality proposals. . . . if I can find a good writer, I'll keep him or her busy."

Happycampers, http://www.happycampers.net
Paginas World Wide Web. Tel.: (505) 439-8293. David Keeney, editor.

Five percent freelance written. This market describes itself as "Your RV Travel Guide to the American Southwest and Northern Mexico. Extensive maps and links to detailed sites. Serves RVers and other road travelers to the region." Established August 1996. Circulation: 150,000. Byline given. Buys permanent Internet rights. Accepts simultaneous and previously published submissions. Pays on publication.

E-mail for queries: editor@happycampers.net.

Editorial Needs: Travel. Query. Word length for articles: 500–1000.

Payment: $50–$75.

Photos/Art: State availability of photos with submission. Pays $5–$10. Buys permanent Internet rights.

Advice from Market: See http://www.happycampers.net/admin/policy.html.

Hardshell, http://www.hardshell.com
Hardshell is an e-book publisher. This market didn't complete our questionnaire, but Mary Wolf in the editorial department did say it qualified to be included in this book. Peruse the site and query before submitting.

E-mail for queries: Mary Wolf at submit@hardshell.com.

Healthlifeatprem.com, http://www.healthlifeatprem.com
PremDotCom, 501 Fifth Ave., Suite 2201, New York, NY 10017. Tel.: (212) 953-2539, fax: (212) 953-2525. M. Dahan, editor/chairman.

"Everything you need to know about your health from nutrition and doctors to beauty tips."

[For full listing see Gardenatprem.com on page 128.]

Hermanmiller.com, http://www.hermanmiller.com
Editorial contact is Christine MacLean.

"Herman Miller, Inc., is a leading multinational provider of office, healthcare, and residential furniture, and furniture management services" that also happens to have content on its site and pays well for that content. (See also Jugglezine, another content column at the Herman Miller site.) Peruse the site and query before submitting. Writers report selling online freelance material to this market. Christine politely declined to complete our questionnaire. Peruse the site and query before submitting.

E-mail for queries: Christine MacLean at christinemaclean@content studio.com.

Homelifeatprem.com, http://www.homelifeatprem.com
PremDotCom, 501 Fifth Ave., Suite 2201, New York, NY 10017. Tel.: (212) 953-2539, fax: (212) 953-2525. M. Dahan, editor/chairman.

"Everything you need to know about your home, about home improvements and repairs, decorating, collectibles, antiques, arts and crafts."

[For full listing see Gardenatprem.com on page 128.]

Houston CitySearch, www.houston.citysearch.com
Ticketmaster Online CitySearch, 790 East Colorado Blvd., Suite 200, Pasadena, CA 91101. Tel.: (626) 405-0050, fax: (626) 405-9929. Michael Phillips, editor.

[For full listing see Atlanta CitySearch on page 97.]

Houston Sidewalk, http://www.houston.sidewalk.com
Microsoft, Lyric Business Centre, 440 Louisiana, Suite 900, Houston, TX 77002. Tel.: (713) 236-7713, fax: (713) 236-7748. John Wilburn, executive producer.

"Guide to arts, entertainment, and shopping in Houston."

E-mail for queries: John Wilburn at jwilburn@microsoft.com.
[For full listing see New York Sidewalk listing on page 78.]

HTMLGoodies, http://www.htmlgoodies.com
EarthWeb's HTMLGoodies gives readers the full range of HTML (HyperText Markup Language) scoop, from beginner starting blocks and basics to "Script Tips" and "Beyond HTML" features such as

DHTML, JavaScripting, and CGI—all the makings for a mightier and more effective Web site. Book reviews and news to boot. For full listing of guidelines, see Developer.com, p. 117.

Hyper, The, http://www.methodfive.com
Methodfive, 632 Broadway, 10th floor, New York, NY 10003. Tel.: (212) 539-0900, fax: (212) 539-0100. Megan Mullins, editor.

Fifty percent freelance written. This market describes itself as "the newsletter for publishing and media professionals interested in the emerging digital culture. 100% unique content. Real analysis, real insight, and relevant reporting." Established May 1998. Circulation: 1500. Pays on publication. Byline given. Inquire about rights.

E-mail for queries: thehyper@methodfive.com.

Editorial Needs: Exposé, interview, opinion, technical, technology, trade. Query. Word length for articles: minimum 500.

Payment: $100–$175.

Advice from Market: "The best freelance writers I've used are those that are familiar with my publication and pitch relevant story ideas. It's a timesaver for me and pretty much ensures that I'll use them for the article."

I.Merchant, http://www.CatalogAgemag.com
Intertec Publishing, 11 River Bend Dr. South, Stamford, CT 06907. Tel.: (203) 358-9900, fax: (203) 358-5823. Laura Beaudry, editorial director.

I.Merchant says it "serves top executives in the electronic catalog markets. Readers are presidents, owners, CEOs, general managers, vice presidents, Webmasters, Web developers, Web marketers, Web merchants." It's a separate quarterly publication featured on the same Web site as Catalog Age. Twenty to 40 percent freelance written. Established 1999. Circulation: withheld. Byline given. Buys worldwide exclusive publication rights for 60 days from first publication, reprint rights, rights to reproduce in other media. Sometimes pays the expenses of writers on assignment. Query.

E-mail for queries: Sherry_Chiger@intertec.com.

Editorial Needs: How-to, technical, technology, company case studies, trends, news stories. Word length for articles: 600–2500.

Payment: varies from $300–$2000. Pays on acceptance.

Photos/Art: Send photos with submission. Negotiates payment individually. Requires identification of subjects. Buys all rights.

Inc. Online: The Web Site for Growing Companies,
http://www.inc.com
Goldhirsh Group, Inc., 38 Commercial Wharf, Boston, MA 02110.
"Please no phone calls or faxes." Leslie Brokaw, editor.

"The premiere online resource for people starting and running their own businesses, Inc. Online includes feature stories and management advice as well as interactive resources including active bulletin boards for trading ideas, searchable business databases, fill-in-the-blanks worksheets, and information organized by business topic." A slim 1 percent freelance written. Established June 1996. (*INC.* magazine was founded in 1979.) Buys all rights.

E-mail for queries: inc.online@inc.com.

Editorial Needs: A handful of freelance writers contribute to the Local Business News area and to Inc. Extra.

Advice from Market: "The bulk of the text at our site comes directly from *INC.* magazine. Almost all of the original editorial content is written by the Inc. Online staff and *INC.* writers."

Industry Standard Online, The, http://www.thestandard.com
Hane Lee, Web editor, (415) 733-5400.

The Industry Standard Online furthers its print counterpart's editorial vision, calling itself "The newsmagazine of the Internet economy." The site is chock full of technology and business content, as well as frequently updated content of its many free e-mail newsletters. Peruse the site and query before submitting.

E-mail for queries: Hane Lee at hanel@thestandard.com.

Inklings: Inkspot's Newsletter for Writers,
http://www.inkspot.com/inklings
Inklings is a free, biweekly electronic newsletter for writers. Its focus is on the craft and business of writing. Debbie Ridpath Ohi, editor in chief. (See page 39 for interview with Debbie Ridpath Ohi.) Seventy-five percent freelance written. Established September 1995. Circulation: over 45,000 subscribers. Pays on publication. Byline given. Purchases

first-time, exclusive, onetime rights, plus nonexclusive archiving rights (back issues of Inklings are kept online). Editorial lead time: 3 months. Accepts simultaneous submissions (if informed) and electronic submissions only. Reports in 2 weeks on queries, 1 month on manuscripts.

Editorial Needs: How-to, interview. Query with published clips. Word length: 250–1000 (average: 800).

Payment: 5 cents/word–10 cents/word for assigned articles; 5 cents/word for unsolicited articles.

E-mail for submissions: submissions@inkspot.com.

Advice from Market: Guidelines are available by autoresponder: guidelines@inkspot.com.

InterfaithFamily.com, http://www.interfaithfamily.com
Jewish Family & Life, 56 Kearney Rd., Needham, MA 02494. Tel.: (781) 449-9894, fax: (781) 449-9825. Ronnie Friedland, managing editor.

This market explains that "InterfaithFamily.com offers a Jewish perspective, respecting the faith of individuals from all religious backgrounds as well as appreciating differences in nationality, race, and culture. While this Web zine will provide information that presents various viewpoints on the wide range of issues and decisions faced by interfaith families, it invites Jewish choices."

[For full listing see GenerationJ.com on page 128.]

ISyndicate, http://www.isyndicate.com
ISyndicate is a new-media take on syndication. Through different options of royalties and ad revenue, it pays freelance writers for all genres of online content. "The amount of revenue depends on how popular your feature becomes" and, according to ISyndicate, popular content leads to "several thousand dollars a month in royalties, and licensing opportunities in other media." Freelancers can submit material on a daily, weekly, monthly, or quarterly basis. Rights-wise, ISyndicate says, "Our customers have limited 'reprint' rights to their content, but their copyright and byline notice will appear every time their content appears on the Web." Your best bet (and our easiest/safest bet) is for you to get the full unadulterated scoop from ISyndicate's Web site, specifically at the self-syndication part: www.isyndicate.com/providers/self_syndications.html. Any subsequent questions can be answered

by Jim Toomey (head of self-syndication) and the ISyndicate crew at content@isyndicate.com.

IT Managers Journal, http://www.ITManagersJournal.com
Andover Advanced Technologies, 50 Nagog Park Rd., 2nd floor, Acton, MA 01720. Tel.: (978) 635-5300, fax: (978) 635-5326. Robin Miller, senior editor.

The IT Managers Journal is a part of the AndoverNews Network and features the daily editorial wisdom of Rod Amis (who has been the "Webslinger for G21: TheWorld's Magazine since March 1996. He has also written user documentation for BBS's and software manuals, and done database development for political campaigns, events management, and personnel companies"). IT has similar topics and links to its parent organization with some technology columns by contributors other than Rod.

E-mail for queries: robin.miller@andover.net

[For full listing see AndoverNews on page 94.]

Jackhammer E-zine, http://www.eggplant-productions.com/jackhammer
Eggplant Productions, 9220 Jill Ln., #2E, Schiller Park, IL 60176. (Eggplant Productions only accepts e-mail submissions.) Tel.: (847) 928-9925. Raechel Henderson, editor.

Ninety-five percent freelance written. "Jackhammer E-zine is a weekly publication of science fiction, fantasy, and horror which explores a Question of the Week. Our audience is truly varied and not limited by age, occupation, or even reading tastes. Jackhammer E-zine really is one of those publications that defies definition." Established December 1997. Circulation: 2000 unique visitors a month. Pays on publication. Byline given. Buys first worldwide electronic rights for pieces never before published on the Internet, worldwide electronic rights for pieces previously published on the Internet. "We purchase these rights up until the time of publication and 90 days after publication. In our contract we ask that the piece bought not be found on the Web at all during that time." Editorial lead time: 1 month. Accepts simultaneous and previously published submissions. Reports in 1 day–2 weeks on queries; 1 day–2 weeks on manuscripts.

E-mail for submissions: jackhammer@eggplant-productions.com.

Editorial Needs: Essays, how-to, humor, fiction, opinion, personal experience, technology. Send complete manuscript. Word length for articles: no minimum–1000 maximum.

Payment: $5–$10.

Photos/Art: State availability of photos with submission. No additional payment. Requires identification of subjects. Buys onetime rights.

Advice from Market: "Guidelines for Jackhammer E-zine can be found at www.eggplant-productions.com/jackhammer/guidelines .html. Please read the guidelines first and then only query if they don't answer your question. I prefer to just see the entire submission rather than answer a query. E-mail all submissions, queries, and comments to jackhammer@eggplant-productions.com. I usually answer within two weeks (usually sooner) on submissions so give me 2 weeks before querying about the status of your submission."

January Magazine: For People Who Like Books,
http://www.janmag.com
Smartypants Studios, #101–1001 W. Broadway, Suite 192, Vancouver, BC V6H 4E4, Canada. "Contact is by e-mail or snail mail only." Linda Richards, editor.

Twenty-five percent freelance written. This market describes itself as "book reviews, author profiles, and interviews." Established November 1997. Circulation: 90,000. Pays on publication. Byline given. Buys First North American electronic. Accepts simultaneous submissions. Reports in 2 weeks on queries, 3 weeks on manuscripts.

E-mail for queries: editor@januarymagazine.com.

Editorial Needs: Interview, book reviews. Query. Word length for articles: 450 minimum.

Payment: $50 (assigned reviews) up to $250 (author profiles/ interviews). "And perhaps getting somewhat higher."

Photos/Art: State availability of photos with submission. Negotiates payment individually. Requires identification of subjects. Buys onetime rights.

Advice from Market: "We are most interested in talking with writers who have the same passion for books that we do. Please take the time to have a good peek around January before querying."

JavaScripts, http://www.javascripts.com
EarthWeb's JavaScripts is true to EarthWeb's tech-savvy site network, combining JavaScript know-how, news, and noisemakers with a bubbling community of like-minded script swappers, free resources, and its own weekly newsletter, "OnFocus!" For full listing of EarthWeb's guidelines, see Developer.com, p. 117.

Jewishfamily.com, http://www.jewishfamily.com
Jewish Family & Life, 56 Kearney Rd., Needham, MA 02494. Tel.: (781) 449-9894, fax: (781) 449-9825. Ronnie Friedland, managing editor.

Jewishfamily.com offers "parenting with purpose," through a wide array of Jewish-related health, holidays, travel, food, blessings, business, and much more.

[For full listing see GenerationJ.com on page 128.]

Journeywoman Online: Connecting women travelers around the world, http://www.journeywoman.com
Evelyn Hannon, editor.

"Your articles should be original. However, they can be female-friendly versions of something you've already written. If this is the case, please note where and when the original article was published."

E-mail: "Don't send your unsolicited articles. Instead e-mail your query letters to: editor@journeywoman.com."

Editorial Needs: "We welcome articles that could fit into the following categories: Love Stories with a Travel Twist, Women-Friendly City Sites, Outdoor Adventures, Personal Travel Stories, Travel 101—How to . . . , Spa Stories, The Older Adventuress. Length: Up to 900 words plus two sidebars dealing with your subject (this is over and above the 900 words). Try to be creative with the type of additional info you provide."

Payment: "Journeywoman is an online co-op of women travelers around the world. As such, we do not pay for each article . . . but we have decided to run an ongoing travel writing competition. Any article that is submitted to us and published in Journeywoman Online within the next competition year (June 1 to May 31) will be eligible for a $200 prize. Best article will be announced in the June issue of Journeywoman Online."

Advice from Market: "Articles should be written from a woman's point of view and should contain information of particular interest to the female traveler. However, we will definitely accept articles from men if they are appropriate to our mandate. We suggest that you read at least two articles posted at our Web site. There is a particular light-hearted spirit and content that we're looking for."

Jugglezine, http://www.jugglezine.com
Jugglezine has a real literary feel to it, featuring long, intelligent essays and a clean design that keeps the writing in the spotlight. This market didn't complete our questionnaire and its contact information seemed to be in flux as this book went to press. (See Hermanmiller.com, its hosting site, for more listing information and alternative contact routes. Also check in with this book's site at www.marketsforwriters .com for more information when it becomes available.) Peruse the site for current editorial contact and send a query before submitting.

Advice from Writers: One writer reports being offered $1/word for "all rights" to a piece, and that those comprehensive rights were impor-tant enough to Jugglezine to finally settle on a higher price per word.

JVibe.com, http://www.jvibe.com
Jewish Family & Life, 56 Kearney Rd., Needham, MA 02494. Tel.: (781) 449-9894, fax: (781) 449-9825. Ronnie Friedland, managing editor.

JVibe is the cool teen representative of the Jewish Family & Life! site network. Flash and Shockwave plug-ins add pizzazz to Yiddish games, sports features and trivia, and a myriad of teen topics with Jewish twists, all dedicated to bringing "together teens from across the globe to bridge the gap of language barriers, geographical boundaries, and religious backgrounds. We hope you can show us how to use tech-nology to unite Jewish youth from around the world. We think you will find new avenues for Jewish expression and a new perspective to explore Jewish culture and opportunities."

[For full listing see GenerationJ.com on page 128.]

Keystrokes, http://www.writelinks.com/keystrokes
Writelinks.com, P.O. Box 142002, Fayetteville, GA 30214. Kate John-ston, managing editor.

Keystrokes is an online magazine about writing, for writers, both published and those to-be-published. One hundred percent freelance written. Established September 1997. Circulation: 7,500. Pays on publication. Byline given. Buys first e-rights for original work, second or reprint e-rights for other work. If the author can show the withdrawal of the piece from the Web is required for publication in another commercial magazine, the author may withdraw the article from the Web site before the 12 months of use is concluded. Accepts simultaneous and previously published submissions. "The editor attempts to report within ten days for both queries and manuscripts. If the writer has not heard in that time, the writer can write the editor and request a report."

E-mail for queries: editor@writelinks.com.

Editorial Needs: How-to, humor, interview, trade, writing-related. Query or send complete manuscript. Word length for articles: "Since this is a Web-based publication, word length isn't as important. We generally respond to this query with 'up to 5000 words.' My personal feeling is the proper length is how long it takes to get the ideas across. This can be 200 words; it can be 1000 words."

Payment: Keystrokes pays $25 per article, assigned or unsolicited, published for the first time. Reprint payments vary from $5 to $20.

Advice from Market: "I expect high-quality writing; I don't want to see something that was poorly written, with poor grammar and lots of spelling errors. I like articles with new slants on the usual topics; new ideas to apply one's writing and get paid for it. Surprise me. See http://www.writelinks.com/keyguide.htm.

Kidshealth.org: Expert Information for Parents, Kids, and Teens from The Nemours Foundation, http://kidshealth.org
The Nemours Center for Children's Health Media, P.O. Box 269, Wilmington, DE 19899. Tel.: (302) 651-4046, fax: (302) 651-4077. Neil Izenberg, M.D., editor in chief.

This market describes itself as a "Web publication on children's health with separate sections aimed at parents, kids (ages 8 to 12), and teens (ages 12 to 18)." Ninety-eight percent freelance written. Established November 1995. Circulation: 400,000. Pays on acceptance. Buys all rights.

E-mail address for resume and clips: Mara Gorman at mgorman@ nemours.org.

Editorial Needs: "This site has hundreds of articles on many topics ranging from infections to development to nutrition to safety. Interested writers should look carefully at the site to see what we are looking for. Articles are assigned by the articles editor. Articles for parents and teens range in length from 1000 to 1500 words; articles for kids are usually 750 words.

Payment: $250–$1500.

Advice from Market: "We do not accept queries from writers who have not written for us before. Interested writers should send a resume and *only* 2 or 3 clips to Mara Gorman, managing editor. Writers do not need to have health-writing experience, but this is a plus. Medical writers should have experience writing for a lay audience. Before expressing their interest, writers should look carefully at the site; we have a very specific tone for each section. When expressing their interest, writers should state their preference as far as audience. Writers should not say they are interested in writing for all 3 sections if they have no experience/training in writing for kids or teens."

Knowledgespace, http://www.knowledgespace.com
KnowledgeSpace, 33 W. Monroe St., 14th floor, Chicago, IL 60603. Tel.: (888) 577-8778. Barbara A. Bohn, managing editor.

Knowledgespace covers topics such as business, taxes, and health care. This market didn't complete our questionnaire, but Barbara Bohn explained its policies: "We don't accept freelance pieces on spec—in other words, we assign a story and then the freelancer produces it, since we already have pretty specific ideas about subject matter and sourcing. Our freelancers all have strong business-news reporting backgrounds. Feel free to drop me a resume, either via e-mail or through the mail." Considering me solely as a freelance writer (and not the author of her listing), Barbara was very courteous and generous with her time, explaining editorial needs and policies.

E-mail for Resumes: barbara.a.bohn@us.arthurandersen.com.

Advice from Market: "If you aren't familiar with the site, you can get a good idea of the kind of work we do by looking at the Hot Issues section of KnowledgeSpace.com."

Advice from Writers: A writer from NWU's database reported that Knowledgespace "will not negotiate" but that the whole process was "painless," and the writer enjoyed $1 per word for Web rights. Another writer reported: "Knowledgespace introduced an abhorrent contract. Initially, they seemed open to change, but the editor candidly and cordially told me that so many writers had signed that the company decided it would do without the writers who wouldn't."

Las Vegas CitySearch, http://www.lasvegas.citysearch.com
Ticketmaster Online CitySearch, 790 East Colorado Blvd., Suite 200, Pasadena, CA 91101. Tel.: (626) 405-0050, fax: (626) 405-9929. Michael Phillips, editor.
[For full listing see Atlanta CitySearch on page 97.]

Literary Trips for Travelers: Following in the Footsteps of Fame, GreatestEscapes.com, Inc., 5255 Gulf Pl., West Vancouver, BC
V7W 2V9, Canada. Victoria Brooks, editor in chief.
"Our Literary Trips for Travelers project brings literature to the world of the traveler. Each story in the anthology follows a particular literary icon through an area or destination made famous by the icon's life or literary works. For example, Victoria Brooks's feature story follows multitalented author/composer Paul Bowles to Tangier, Morocco. All stories collected in the anthology are written by professional writers." Seventy-five percent freelance written. Circulation depends on sales—"It's to be a print book and sold separately on the Internet at www.greatestescapes.com." Pays on acceptance. Byline given. Buys exclusive e-rights and onetime print rights. Accepts simultaneous and previously published submissions. Reports in 1 month on queries, six months on manuscripts.
    E-mail for queries: editor@greatestescapes.com.
    Editorial Needs: Book excerpts, essays, travel. Query with published clips. Word length for articles: Minimum 2000–4000.
    Payment for assigned articles: "Lit Trips project: Writers whose stories (accompanied by pictures) are accepted for the Literary Trips for Travelers project will be paid a minimum of $200 (reprinted stories/articles) to a maximum of $350 (new unpublished story). Once paid, writers will provide GreatestEscapes.com with nonexclusive print

rights, in all languages, throughout the world. Furthermore, writers will provide GreatestEscapes.com with exclusive online rights for the text only. The complete anthology will be sold in bookstores across North America, but individual stories will also be sold over the Internet. Writers will receive a royalty generated by each on-line sale of the individual story (the exact royalty percentage is yet to be determined)."

Photos/Art: State availability of photos with submission, no additional payment. Requires captions, model releases. Buys onetime rights.

Advice from Market: "Please e-mail assist@home.com and request lit trip guidelines."

Maiden Voyages Online, Travel and Transformation for Women, http://www.maiden-voyages.com
109 Minna St., Suite 240, San Francisco, CA 94105. Fax: (510) 528-5163. Nanette C-Lee, editor.

This market describes itself as "a consumer magazine for women who love to travel or who dream about travel—tips, destinations, safety suggestions, cross-cultural communication, and a Traveling Woman's Forum." Established March 1996. Twenty-five percent freelance written. Circulation: 1,000. Pays on publication. Byline given. Buys first North American, second serial, all rights for "traveling solo in" articles. Accepts previously published submissions. Reports in 4–6 months on manuscripts.

No e-mail submissions or queries. Send via regular mail to the above address. "My e-mail gets clogged with unsolicited e-mail submissions. If I have contact with a writer then they can submit via e-mail. Otherwise, I'm wading through hundreds of e-mails every day. No fun."

Editorial Needs: Health/fitness, historical, travel, sports, women's. "Traveling Solo in" (for specific countries). See online guidelines. Send complete manuscript. Word length for articles: 2000 maximum.

Payment: $25–$50 depending upon editing required.

Photos/Art: State availability of photos with submission. Negotiates payment individually. Requires captions, model releases. Buys onetime rights.

Advice from Market: "I don't need any new submissions [at press time for this book]. I will be asking for specifics on the Web site writers' page (http://www.maiden-voyages.com/info.html). Unless you

experienced something that changed your life or your perceptions of
the world, don't bother sending in the story. Travel stories can be like
vacation photos. I'm looking for the unique experience, not the one
that puts your guests to sleep."

Mex Connect, http://www.mexconnect.com
This book's senior contributing writer Karen Morrissey explains, "If
Mexico is your area of expertise, Mexconnect is the market to
approach. It includes sections on the arts, cooking, history, travel, poli-
tics, and many others." This market didn't complete our question-
naire, but writers have reported selling it online freelance material.
Peruse the site and query before submitting.
   E-mail for queries: mexwrite@mexconnect.com.

Miami CitySearch, http://www.miami.citysearch.com
Ticketmaster Online CitySearch, 790 East Colorado Blvd., Suite 200,
Pasadena, CA 91101. Tel.: (626) 405-0050, fax: (626) 405-9929. Michael
Phillips, editor.
   [For full listing see Atlanta CitySearch on page 97.]

Mind's Eye Fiction, http://tale.com
Mind's Eye Fiction, 15231 Silverman, Webster, TX 77598. "Submissions
and editorial correspondence by e-mail only. Use postal address only
for signed contracts." Tel.: (281) 280-9129. Ken Jenks, editor in chief.
   This market describes itself as "short stories, novellas, novelettes,
and novels targeted at adult readers." Eighty percent freelance written.
Established December 1995. Circulation: 167,000. Byline given, with
author's e-mail and URL. Buys nonexclusive electronic rights. Reprints
cheerfully accepted. Contract can be canceled at any time. Accepts
simultaneous and previously published submissions. Reports in 1
month on queries, 3 months on manuscripts.
   E-mail for submissions: MindsEye@tale.com.
   Editorial Needs: Humor, fiction—prose fiction only. Send complete
manuscript. Word length for articles: 1500 and up.
   Payment: "It's complicated, but the gist of it is that we pay a 75 percent royalty on all pay-per-view and advertising revenue generated by
the author's story for as long as the story is online. Varies widely, from

$1 per month to $20 per month per story or novel. See http://tale .com/writech.phtml for details."

Photos/Art: Send photos with submission. No additional payment. Buys same rights as for content.

Advice from Market: See tale.com/writech.phtml.

Mktx.com, http://www.mktx.com
Cheryl Coupe, editor of the site's online newsletter.

This book's senior contributing writer Karen Morrissey explains, "Marketing Architects combines 'creativity, pragmatism and technical insight" to meet your company's business objectives.' The site offers numerous services ranging from direct and internet marketing to content development and public relations." Peruse the site and query before submitting.

E-mail for queries: Cheryl Coupe at cheryl@mktx.com.

Molson.com, http://www.molson.com
This is basically a branded men's magazine. Beer, sports, music, man stuff. This market didn't complete our questionnaire, but writers report that it has paid freelancers for online writing. Peruse the site and query before submitting.

E-mail for queries: jxesposi@molson.com.

MoneyLife Channel: IVillage, http://www.ivillagemoneylife.com/
iVillage: The Women's Network, 170 Fifth Ave., New York, NY 10010. Fax: (212) 604-9133. Kellie Krumplitsch, editorial director.

IVillage's MoneyLife channel keeps true to iVillage's penchant for helping readers with how-to's. Money management is considered as a tool to help readers rise above debt issues and realize their dreams. Sections include investment, banking, insurance, and taxes.

E-mail for queries: Lisa Kraynak at lkraynak@mail.ivillage.com. [For full listing see Parent Soup on page 157.]

Monster.com, http://www.monster.com
Eileen O'Reilly, content director.

Monster.com offers an e-mail newsletter, advice columns, and apropos features covering all aspects of the career search. This market didn't complete our questionnaire, but writers report that it pays for online freelance material. Peruse the site and query before submitting.

E-mail for queries: eoreilly@monster.com.

Payment: $1 per word.

Advice from Writers: "They are wonderful. Interesting, efficient, professional, and talented. And they pay well—around $1 a word, depending on the assignment, writer's experience, etc."

MP3.com, http://www.mp3.com

10350 Science Center Dr., San Diego, CA 92121. Doug Reece, senior editor.

As reported at Writersmarkets.com, "MP3.com is a digital music hub." Circulation: 6 million. Buys onetime electronic rights. Pays one month after publication. Peruse the site and query before submitting.

E-mail for queries: Doug Reece at doug@mp3.com.

Payment: 20 cents per word. Word length for articles: "Depends on section and story." Query.

Advice from Market: "We need writers with a knowledge of music and/or technology and how technology is impacting the music business." Welcomes new writers.

MSNBC on the Internet: Business,

Tel.: (425) 703-9556. John Flinn, editor.

Peruse the site before querying, and preferably query only if you've written for comparable markets.

E-mail for queries: John.Flinn@msnbc.com.

[For full listing see MSNBC on the Internet: Sports on page 149.]

MSNBC on the Internet: Health

Tel.: (201) 583-5862. Charlene Laino, editor.

Peruse the site before querying, and preferably query only if you've written for comparable markets.

E-mail for queries: Charlene.Laino@msnbc.com.

[For full listing see MSNBC on the Internet: Sports on page 149.]

MSNBC on the Internet: Living·Travel

Laura Tuchman, editor.

Please note that Living·Travel editor Laura Tuchman has only "very limited freelance needs" and "cannot respond to any outside freelance inquiries" at the time this book went to press. Aka, she's very busy, understandably so. Peruse the site before querying, and preferably query only if you've written for comparable markets.

E-mail for queries: Laura.tuchman@msnbc.com. See above caveats.

[For full listing see MSNBC on the Internet: Sports below.]

MSNBC on the Internet: News

Tel.: (425) 703-4090. Dean Wright, editor.

Peruse the site before querying, and preferably query only if you've written for comparable markets.

E-mail for queries: Dean.Wright@msnbc.com.

[For full listing see MSNBC on the Internet: Sports below.]

MSNBC on the Internet: Opinion

Joan Connell, editor.

Peruse the site before querying, and preferably query only if you've written for comparable markets. Please note that Joan is exceptionally busy and has made it quite clear that, as this book goes to press, she "really would not welcome new submissions from writers not already under contract." Maybe she's less busy now; she probably isn't.

E-mail for queries: Joan.Connell@msnbc.com. See above caveats.

[For full listing see MSNBC on the Internet: Sports below.]

MSNBC on the Internet Sports,

http://www.msnbc.com/news/SPT_Front.asp?a

MSNBC on the Internet, One Microsoft Way, Bldg. 25, Redmond, WA 98052. Tel.: (425) 936-1960, fax: (425) 703-0415. Danny DeFreitas, executive sports editor.

This market describes itself as "national sports news; our audience is mostly male 18–50 years old." Established August 1995. Circulation: withheld. Pays on acceptance. Byline given. Buys wire rights. Accepts previously published submissions. Ten percent freelance written.

E-mail for queries: spteds@msnbc.com.

Editorial Needs: Opinion, sports. Query or query with published clips. Word length for articles: 1500.

Payment: Usual range is $150–$300. Sometimes pays the expenses of writers on assignment.

Advice from Market: "Since we are a national Web site, we are interested in sports news stories and features that have a broad national interest. We don't run outdoors articles and as a rule aren't interested in nonrevenue college sports. If you have something that you think we might be interested in publishing, contact us first through e-mail or phone call."

Nashville CitySearch, www.nashville.citysearch.com
Ticketmaster Online CitySearch, 790 East Colorado Blvd., Suite 200, Pasadena, CA 91101. Tel.: (626) 405-0050, fax: (626) 405-9929. Nashville office tel.: (615) 259-3990. Michael Phillips, editor.

[For full listing see Atlanta CitySearch on page 97.]

Nationalgeographic.com, http://www.nationalgeographic.com
National Geographic Society, 1145 17th St., N.W., Washington, DC 20036. Tel.: (202) 857-7000. Valerie May, managing editor.

This market describes itself as "interactive features, photo galleries, forums, news site, education site, travel, NG store, maps, promotion and editorial content for NGM, World, Traveler, Adventure, Books, TV." Established June 1997. Circulation: 1.5 million. Twenty percent freelance written. Pays on acceptance. Byline given.

E-mail for queries only ("unsolicited submissions are not welcome"): editor@nationalgeographic.com.

Editorial Needs: Book excerpts, entertainment, essays, health/ fitness, general interest, historical, interview, music, new product, personal experience, technology, travel, sports. Query with published clips.

Payment: "Varies according to type of article and writer's experience. Range is more or less 30 cents to $1 a word. Length of articles depends entirely upon the type of feature." Sometimes pays the expenses of writers on assignment.

Photos/Art: State availability of photos with submission or send photos with submission. Requires captions, model releases, identification of subjects.

Advice from Market: "Let me reiterate, we do not encourage unsolicited [submissions]. Queries may be addressed to editor@national geographic.com."

Neverworlds: Unique Fiction, http://www.neverworlds.com
Kevin L. McPherson, chief editor.

"All submissions we've received so far have been from unpublished or freelance writers." Neverworlds was designed to showcase the much-underrated work of up-and-coming writers (and artists!), and is aimed at anyone interested in experiencing the best in today's new fiction." Established: April 1998. Circulation: 1000. Pays on publication. Byline given. "We purchase first electronic rights. For more details see our [guidelines]." Accepts previously published submissions. Reports in 1 week on queries, 3 months on manuscripts. ["No mailing address. E-mails only."]

E-mail for submissions: editor@neverworlds.com or dechaune@ ns.sympatico.ca.

Editorial Needs: Entertainment, fiction, interview, poetry, technology. Send complete manuscript. Word length for articles: 1000–10,000.

Payment: $5–$30.

Photos/Art: State availability of art with submission. Send art with submission. Pays $5–$30. Buys onetime rights.

Advice from Market: Guidelines at http://www3.ns.sympatico.ca/ dechaune/neverworlds/subs.htm.

New City, http://www.newcity.com
Frank Sennet, editor.

This book's senior contributing writer Karen Morrissey explains that "Newcity.com deems itself 'your gateway to Alternative America' offering 'perspectives on news and culture you won't find at your local newsstand—or anywhere else, for that matter.' Edgy articles on sex, subcultures, and surfing are among the alternatives available for your clicking." Peruse the site and query before submitting.

E-mail for queries: frank@newcity.com.

New York CitySearch, http://www.newyork.citysearch.com
Ticketmaster Online CitySearch, 790 East Colorado Blvd., Suite 200,

Pasadena, CA 91101. Tel.: (626) 405-0050, fax: (626) 405-9929. New York office tel.: (212) 647-5700.

[For full listing see Atlanta Citysearch on page 97.]

New York Sidewalk, http://www.newyork.sidewalk.com
[See full listing on page 78 in "Top Ten Places to be Published Online."]

New York Times on the Web, http://www.nytimes.com
[See full listing on page 80 in "Top Ten Places to be Published Online."]

New York Today, http:/www.nytoday.com
Elliott Rebhun, editor.

This book's contributing writer, Marisa Lowenstein, explains that "In the spirit of Sidewalk.com and CitySearch.com, the New York Times steps up to the plate with NYtoday.com, an informative and semi-hip guide to the myriad happenings in the busy Big Apple. When the Times deliver, it delivers big! No category is left untouched by this detailed and diverse guide to the big, bad city. Viewers are instantly greeted by NYtoday's events of the day, which can vary from pricey Manhattan art exhibits and Lincoln Center dance performances to fluffy primetime TV shows and rollerblade disco parties in Brooklyn. Although the calendar seems to be the focal point, the site also has an extensive menu of urban categories (entertainment, life, community, neighborhood—to name a few) with subcategories catering to both the overstimulated NYC native ("Getaways") and the overwhelmed NYC tourist ("Hotels"). New York City is all about activities and NYtoday is all about reviewing them. If there's a movie, restaurant opening, play or concert you should know about, NYtoday is going to tell you about it. And while NYtoday definitely dares to venture into the dark reaches of downtown youth culture, the tone of the site is tempered by its newspaper big brother, keeping it consistently close to its more mainstream roots." This market didn't complete our questionnaire, but Elliot Rebhun says NYtoday.com does buy online freelance material—about 40 percent of the site is freelance written—and that they don't work with new writers. Peruse the site and query before submitting.

E-mail for queries: submissions@nytimes.com.

Officelifeatprem.com, http://www.officelifeatprem.com
PremDotCom, 501 Fifth Ave., Suite 2201, New York, NY 10017. Tel.: (212) 953-2539, fax: (212) 953-2525. M. Dahan, editor/chairman.

"Everything you need to know about the office—aimed at small business offices and the small home office market featuring office equipment and furniture and other supplies."

[For full listing see Gardenatprem.com on page 128.]

Off Road, http://www.off-road.com
Norm Lenhart, managing editor.

Your virtual off-road vehicle fest. Fast, adventurous, engine-powered. No pavement. You get the picture. Off-Road.com affirms itself as "your best source of information for all off-road vehicle activities. 4×4, four-wheel-drive trucks and SUVs, Jeeps, ATVs, dirt bikes and off-road motorcycles, snowmobiles, dunebuggies and sand rails, automobiles, racing, and more. We have trail info, tech, photo galleries, product news and reviews, projects, stories—just about anything about off-roading!" Peruse the site and query before submitting.

E-mail for queries: Norm Lenhart at lenhart@off-road.com.

Advice from Writers: One freelancer reported being able to secure $2 per word for an article.

OnMoney, http://www.onmoney.com
Ameritrade. Curtis Lang, editor.

At press time for this book, OnMoney was still in beta testing, poised to be launched and viewed. We do know it's funded and focused on money/personal finance with helpful how-to's, and the tag line of "Your online financial assistant." Check in with http://www.markets forwriters.com for the full scoop and contact information once it becomes available. This market didn't complete our questionnaire, but writers report that it does pay for online freelance material. Peruse the site and query before submitting.

E-mail for queries: clang@onmoney.com.

Advice from Writers: "The editor, Curtis Lang, is wonderful to work with—kind, knowledgeable, talented, and helpful. The pay isn't bad and depends on the writer's experience. They've got some interesting things planned."

Orato: True Stories from Real People, http://www.orato.com
Acher International, Suite 400–525, Seymour St., Vancouver, BC V6B 3H7, Canada. Tel.: (604) 608-1070, fax: (604) 605-8262. Charles Montgomery, editor.

Ninety percent freelance written. "Orato is an online magazine concept offering a dynamic alternative to traditional media. It will present vivid first-person stories from people involved in or affected by current events. Those narratives will be complemented with hard facts, strong photography, and documentary video. Equal parts magazine and talk show, Orato will use the unique power of the Internet to make readers a part of every story." Established October 1999. Circulation: not available yet. "We pay ⅓ on acceptance and ⅔ on publication." Byline given. Buys exclusive publication rights for 60 days from date of publication in Orato, and the right to license or syndicate.

E-mail for queries: editor@orato.com.

Editorial Needs: Book excerpts, historical, inspirational, interview, personal experience, teen, travel, sports, women's. "We need first-person stories from people involved in or affected by current events." Query. "Or better, register as a contributor using the forms at http://www.orato.com." Word length for articles: 300–2000.

Payment: $100–$400, "but we will occasionally pay much more for 'marquee-value' subjects. Unless otherwise agreed upon, we'll pay you 25 percent of any payments we receive for [licensing or syndication of your work]. If we can't run a story for any reason, we offer a kill fee of 30 percent of the agreed contributor's fee."

Photos/Art: Send photos with submission. Negotiates payment individually. Requires captions and identification of subjects. Buys all rights (but not exclusive use).

Advice from Market: "The contributors' site at http://www.orato .com is an illustration of where we're headed and a call to action for prospective writers. Here you'll find examples of the kind of stories we want and information on how you can contribute to Orato. Orato is interested in first-person stories that will inspire, anger, and delight readers, while lending a cold shot of truth and meaning to issues of the day. We need true stories from people behind current issues, events and trends, or stories from ordinary people who have had extraordinary experiences. We need professional-quality photos for every story, and will add audio/video clips whenever available. The key to our concept, though, is first-person storytelling. Our readers are more interested in narrative than opinion, and they don't want it secondhand. This poses a challenge to writers submitting stories about other people. Remember, you are transcribing your subjects' words and helping them tell their stories to the world. In essence, each feature will be one big quote, edited for brevity, vitality and libel. We aren't interested in stories sullied by our correspondents' values or sense of fairness, whether justified or not. Instead, to balance those first-person rants, we'll include short, newsy sidebars with each feature, giving details about the story subject and enough context for readers to form their own opinions."

Orlando CitySearch, http://www.orlando.citysearch.com
Ticketmaster Online CitySearch, 790 East Colorado Blvd., Suite 200, Pasadena, CA 91101. Tel.: (626) 405-0050, fax: (626) 405-9929. Michael Phillips, editor.
[For full listing see Atlanta CitySearch on page 97.]

Orphic Chronicle, The, http://www.orphic-chronicle.com
The Orphic Chronicle, P.O. Box 171202, Arlington, TX 76003-1202. S. Kay Elmore, editor.
"This is a Web zine dedicated to speculative fiction, horror, and fantasy, recommended for mature readers. In addition to fiction and poetry, we offer interviews, book reviews, and a growing celebrity autograph section for fans." Eighty percent freelance written. Established October 1996. Circulation: 1000. Pays on publication. Byline given. Buys either first worldwide electronic rights or onetime rights for reprints. Accepts previously published submissions. Reports immediately on queries, 6–8 weeks on manuscripts.
E-mail for submissions: editor@orphic-chronicle.com

Editorial Needs: Fiction, interview, poetry, feature articles on SF/horror notable celebrities. Query for nonfiction; send complete manuscript for fiction/poetry.

Payment: $5 for unpublished work, or ¼ cent per word, whichever is greater. $2.50 for published work or ⅛ cent per word, whichever is greater. Poetry: $5 unpublished, $2.50 published, flat rate. Nonfiction pays the same as fiction rates.

Photos/Art: Send photos with submission. Negotiates payment individually. Requires model releases. Buys onetime rights.

Advice from Market: See www.orphic-chronicle.com/guide.htm.

Parenting Today's Teen, http://www.parentingteens.com
Kayena Communications, P.O. Box 600144, San Diego, CA 92160. Tel.: (619) 229-0199, fax: (619) 229-0197. Diana Kathrein, publisher and editor in chief.

Thirty percent freelance written. "Parenting Today's Teen, an online publication, strives to bridge the gap between parents and teens. We offer resources, insight, support, and inspiration to the parent and teen community. Our reader base consists of parents, teens, professionals, educators, and administrators." Established September 1996. Circulation 25,000. Pays on publication. Byline given. Buys first North American serial rights and onetime Internet rights. Accepts previously published submissions. Reports in 1–2 weeks on queries and manuscripts.

E-mail address for editorial submissions: Frances Reza, managing editor, at FrncesReza@aol.com.

Editorial Needs: Essays, how-to, humor, general interest, inspirational, music, opinion, personal experience, teen. Query. Word length for articles: 400–1200.

Payment: $10–$25.

Photos/Art: State availability of photos with submission, no additional. Requires captions, model releases, identification of subjects. Buys onetime rights.

Advice from Market: "Guidelines can be found on our Web site at www.parentingteens.com/guidelines.html. We prefer queries over completed manuscripts. Before querying read and become familiar with our e-zine and the topics we've already addressed. Please, no poetry or fiction submissions. We are easy to approach and invite new/unpublished writers."

Parent Soup, http://www.parentsoup.com
iVillage, 170 Fifth Ave., New York, NY 10010. Fax: (212) 604-9133. Linda Osborne, programming director.

"Parent Soup is the #1 online community for parents." Ten percent freelance written. Established January 1996. Circulation: 2 million. Pays on acceptance. Byline given. Buys negotiated rights. Accepts simultaneous submissions, previously published submissions. Reports in two weeks on queries and manuscripts.

E-mail for queries: PSeditor@mail.ivillage.com.

Editorial Needs: Book excerpts, humor, personal experience, essays, inspirational, interview/profile, historical/nostalgic. Query with published clips or send complete manuscript. Length: 200–1500 words. Articles focus on information for parents of all ages, from expecting parents to grandparents.

Payment: Negotiates payment individually.

Advice from Market: "Please be familiar with Parent Soup before submitting article ideas. We are interested in either humor or educating parents about all things concerning the family, including but not limited to health, education, activities, finance, sports, parenting styles, entertainment, technology, holidays, and the ages and stages of children."

PC World Online, http://www.pcworld.com
PC World Communications Inc., 501 Second St., Suite 600, San Francisco, CA 94107. Tel.: (415) 243-0500, fax: (415) 442-1891. Phillip Lemmons, editorial director.

This market describes itself as "PC news, reviews, and how-to information for PC-proficient business managers." Established 1995. Seventy percent freelance written. Circulation: withheld. Pays on publication. Byline given. Reports in 1 month on queries. "No obligation to respond on manuscripts."

E-mail for queries: webmaster@pcworld.com.

Editorial Needs: Technology. Query with published clips. Word length for articles: 500–6000.

Payment: 50 cents per word–75 cents per word. Sometimes pays the expenses of writers on assignment.

Photos/Art: State availability of photos with submission. Negotiates rights and payment individually. Requires model releases, identification of subjects.

Advice from Market: "Keep queries short and make sure that they are on target for our audience. It helps to demonstrate that you've read some stories from the site."

Petlifeatprem.com, http://www.petlifeatprem.com
PremDotCom, 501 Fifth Ave., Suite 2201, New York, NY 10017. Tel.: (212) 953-2539, fax: (212) 953-2525. M. Dahan, editor/chairman.

"Everything you need to know about your pets, tips on looking after them and products to purchase for them."

[For full listing see Gardenatprem.com on page 128.]

Pets Channel: IVillage http://www.ivillage.com/pets
iVillage: The Women's Network, 170 Fifth Ave., New York, NY 10010. Fax: (212) 604-9133. Kellie Krumplitsch, editorial director.

IVillage's Pets Channel focuses on dogs and cats, though birds make their way into the site known as "the place for people who love their pets." And love they do—this site is a pet pride free-for-all. Content includes pet photos, videos, chats, naming database, and numerous columns offering tips and tricks for making pet care easy and enjoyable.

E-mail for queries: Dan Leeds at dleeds@mail.ivillage.com.

[For full listing see Parent Soup on page 157.]

Philadelphia CitySearch, http://www.philadelphia.citysearch.com
Ticketmaster Online CitySearch, 790 East Colorado Blvd., Suite 200, Pasadena, CA 91101. Tel.: (626) 405-0050, fax: (626) 405-9929. Michael Phillips, editor.

[For full listing see Atlanta CitySearch on page 97.]

Phoenix CitySearch, http://www.phoenix.citysearch.com
Ticketmaster Online CitySearch, 790 East Colorado Blvd., Suite 200,

Pasadena, CA 91101. Tel.: (626) 405-0050, fax: (626) 405-9929. Michael Phillips, editor.

[For full listing see Atlanta CitySearch on page 97.]

Phys: Fitness for the Mind, Body and Spirit, http://www.phys.com CondéNet Inc., 140 East 45th St., 37th floor, New York, NY 10017. (Note: at press time for book, CondéNet may be moving to 342 Madison Avenue. Be sure to confirm address.) Tel.: (212) 880-4612, fax: (212) 880-8499. Rosanne Lufrano, editor in chief.

Seventy-five percent freelance written. "Phys is a health and wellness service that smart women turn to for the best and latest health information, personalized tools and advice. Authoritative text and expertly crafted interactive features combine with a lively, clean design to offer the means women need to create and follow health programs that fit their lives and lifestyles. Phys features a mix of original material and content adapted from Condé Nast publications, including *Self, Glamour, Mademoiselle, Allure, Vogue,* and *Women's Sports and Fitness,* as well as a variety of tools which help users manage their own health and fitness needs. The service aims to give its audience of professional women in their twenties, thirties, and forties advice they can use. Whether it be calculating body mass index, making the most of your metabolism, or learning how to stretch, Phys uniquely integrates its information into the personal experience." Established August 1996. Circulation: 800,000. Pays on acceptance. Byline given sometimes. Buys all rights.

E-mail for queries: rlufrano@condenet.com.

Editorial Needs: Health/fitness, how-to, general interest, interview, new product, opinion, personal experience, travel, sports, women's, pregnancy/babies, astrology. Query with published clips. Word length for articles: 200–500 or 500 per Web page (depends on structure).

Payment: $500–$2000. Sometimes pays the expenses of writers on assignment.

Photos/Art: State availability of photos with submission. Negotiates payment individually. Requires captions, model releases, identification of subjects. Buys all rights.

Advice from Market: "We don't have online guidelines. Everything we publish is by assignment; however, we entertain pitches that may turn into an assignment. Phys is a site about service. Everything we do—whether it's creating a calculator or starting a forum or publishing an article—has to provide value to our audience, allowing them to take away some knowledge that they can apply to their life, goals, and lifestyle. We do not tend to publish lengthy articles or articles that are introspective. We endeavor to personalize the experience for the user. Features with interactive components are useful, as well as features that can incorporate aspects of community-building. A good Phys-worthy piece can be organized into a group of Web pages or components. Another positive aspect would be if a feature allows the user to get a glimpse into the subject matter and then if they decide to, they can go deeper. It is also good if a piece can add value to an existing strong feature at Phys—a new calculator, or more guide material on a physical activity/sport that we cover in the Fitness area, a package on a particular vitamin/herb that can be added to our vitamin database in Nutrition/Eating Well."

Pif Magazine, http://www.pifmagazine.com
Pif, PMB 248, 4820 Yelm Hwy. SE, Suite B, Lacey, WA 98503-4903. Tel.: (615) 463-8867. Camille Renshaw, senior editor.

"Pif is a monthly literary magazine, published strictly online. Its sections include fine poetry, fiction, micro fiction, book reviews, film reviews, music reviews, zine reviews, and other commentary. Past writers have included Amy Hempel, David Lehman, and Richard Weems. The magazine includes a strictly literary link exchange, called "Zine-X," and the largest literary search engine online, called Pilot-Search.com. It is the "Starting Point for the Literary e-Press." Established October 1995. One hundred percent freelance written. Circulation: 50,000. Pays on publication. Byline given. Buys first publication rights. Note: "No previously published, unsolicited submissions are accepted." Reports in 2 weeks on queries. "Immediate acknowledgement of receipt of submissions; within 1 month regarding acceptance/rejection."

E-mail for poetry: poetry@pifmagazine.com.
E-mail for commentary: commentary@pifmagazine.com.
E-mail for fiction: fiction@pifmagazine.com.
E-mail for general contact: editor@pifmagazine.com.

Editorial Needs: Book excerpts, essays, humor, fiction, general interest, interview, music, opinion, personal experience, poetry, technology, travel—"but all of these must have a 'literary' spin in terms of content or quality of writing style." Query with published clips or send complete manuscript. Word length for articles: 500–2500.

Payment: "Usual range [is] $5–$250." Sometimes pays the expenses of writers on assignment.

Photos/Art: Freelancers should send photos with submission. No additional payment. Buys onetime rights.

Advice from Market: See http://www.pifmagazine.com/rules.shtml.

Playboy.com, http://www.playboy.com

This is *Playboy*'s online version, with the same content that makes the print version the number one men's magazine in the country. "Hot topics" range from music, movies, and travel to staples such as sex and relationships, with a little "breaking news" to boot. Peruse the site and query before submitting. An associate editor at the print magazine suggested, "If you want to find out about online writing opportunities, you should direct your query to Rodger Brown."

E-mail for queries: rodgerb@playboy.com.

Portland CitySearch, http://www.portland.citysearch.com

Ticketmaster Online CitySearch, 790 East Colorado Blvd., Suite 200, Pasadena, CA 91101. Tel.: (626) 405-0050, fax: (626) 405-9929. Portland office tel.: (503) 225-0123. Michael Phillips, editor.

[For full listing see Atlanta CitySearch on page 97.]

Princeton Review Online, http://www.review.com

The Princeton Review, 2315 Broadway, New York, NY 10024. Edgar Lopez, editorial director, Online Services.

"Princeton Review Online offers information about standardized tests, college and graduate-school admissions, internships, careers, and lots more. Students can find the right college or grad school with our customizable search engines, and they can even determine their chances for acceptance at a variety of schools. Our audience is college-bound high schoolers, their parents, and anyone applying to graduate, medical, law, or business school." Established 1994. Twenty percent freelance written. Circulation: 1 million. Pays on acceptance. Byline given sometimes. Editorial lead time: 2 weeks to 1 month. Accepts simultaneous submissions. Reports on queries and manuscripts within two weeks. Buys all rights.

E-mail for queries: webeditor@review.com.

Editorial Needs: Personal experience, essays, interview/profile, general interest, opinion. Query with published clips. Word length: 100–1000.

Payment: 50 cents per word. Sometimes pays expenses of writers on assignment.

Advice from Market: "Write in first person or about real-life stuff, with sidebars (or links) to fill in the background or related info. For example, we had a piece about transferring colleges. The writer interviewed 10 people to get their stories: why they transferred, how they chose a new place, if it was better or worse, etc. His sidebar was the 12 Steps to Transferring Colleges."

Promo, http://www.promomagazine.com
Intertec Publishing, 11 River Bend Dr. South, Stamford, CT 06907. Tel.: (203) 358-9900, fax: (203) 358-5823. Al Urbanski, editor.

Promo explains that it's "the only magazine dedicated solely to covering the $79 billion promotion marketing industry. Promo supplies readers with news, trends, and 'how-to' information," with topics ranging from ad specialties, alternative media, and in-store marketing to promotion research and specialty events.

E-mail for queries: Naczu@aol.com.

[For full listing see Catalog Age on page 106.]

Pulp City, http://www.pulpcity.com/done/pulpcity.html
"Pulp City is an online fiction area, where users go for entertainment and information. It features serialized fiction with quality graphics and high-end multimedia. Pulp City also serves as a valuable resource for aspiring writers by providing information on other online fiction sites, writers' events or seminars and editorials and updates on online fiction development. Unpublished writers are welcome." Peruse the site and query before submitting.

E-mail for queries: "If you are interested in submitting work or want more information, please contact the Pulp City Editor! (editor@pulp city.com)."

Quill Magazine, The: The quarterly e-zine for beginning writers, http://www.thequill.com
Austin Aerospace Ltd., 2900 Warden Ave., P.O. Box 92207, Toronto, Ontario M1W 3Y0, Canada. Tel.: (416) 410-0277, fax: (416) 497-6737. Charlotte Austin, editor.

"The Quill Magazine quarterly is an electronic publication dedicated to the issues of importance to beginning writers, from the simple query letter to specific how-to writing techniques. Our readership is international, our audience is sophisticated and well informed. The Quill favors a particular writing style that is informative, concise, and entertaining. Established August 1998. One hundred percent freelance written. Circulation: 20,000. Pays on acceptance. Byline given. Buys first exclusive electronic rights, and archive rights for one year. Reports in 1 week on queries, 2 weeks on manuscripts.

E-mail for queries: austin@thequill.com.

Editorial Needs: How-to, fiction, interview. Query. Word length for articles: 800–1200.

Payment: $50–$60.

Advice from Market: "Read the free sample issue available on our Web site. Subscribe to the magazine to gain an understanding of what we are about. Don't query or submit blindly. The Quill concentrates on a specific niche market and focuses entirely on the concerns of beginning writers. We publish short fiction pieces from new writers, how-to articles on the craft of writing, columns on the technical side of writing, book reviews and interviews, paying markets open to beginning writers. We don't publish poetry, essays, personal experience, travel or health articles. Consult and adhere to published guidelines. Query first with a well-developed idea and article slant. Be specific, know what you want to say, and then say it well."

Recursive Angel, http://www.recursiveangel.com
Aslan Enterprises, 272 Osborne Hill Rd., Fishkill, NY 12524. Tel.: (914) 896-5984, fax: (914) 765-1157. David Hunter Sutherland, managing editor.

"Recursive Angel is one of the first creative writing/arts publications to have made its presence on the Internet. We feature cutting-edge fiction, poetry, and art, and have received noteworthy commentary from the New York Times on the Web, *The Boston Review*, Poets & Writers, and many others. Our goal is to continue to find and publish the best new writers of today and tomorrow." Established October 1991. One hundred percent freelance written. Circulation: 16,000. Pays on publication. Buys first rights. Accepts simultaneous submissions. Reports in 2 weeks to 1 month on queries and manuscripts.

E-mail for administration: David Sutherland at dsutherland@calldei.com.

E-mail for poetry submissions: Gene Doty at gdoty@umr.edu or CK Tower at vixxen@sojourn.com.

E-mail for fiction submissions: Paul Kloppenborg at paulk@library.lib.rmit.edu.au.

E-mail for art submissions: recangel@calldei.com.

Editorial Needs: Fiction, poetry, art. Send complete ms. Sometimes pays the expenses of writers on assignment. Word length for articles: fiction, 1500; poetry, 40 lines maximum; art, size varies.

Payment: Poetry: $10 per piece; poetry w/RealAudio recording: $15; fiction: $15 per piece; art negotiated at time of acceptance (minimum $30). "Oh, and of course you can check our pay rates out at: http://www.RecursiveAngel.com/pay.htm."

Photos/Art: State availability of photos with submission. Negotiates payment individually. Requires identification of subjects. Buys onetime rights.

Advice from Market: "It can't be overstated that future contributors should follow the guidelines to a T. This, in essence, increases the chances of having the work properly read and reviewed."

Relationships Channel: IVillage,

http://www.ivillage.com/relationships
iVillage: The Women's Network, 170 Fifth Ave., New York, NY 10010. Fax: (212) 604-9133. Kellie Krumplitsch, editorial director.

IVillage's Relationships channel says it's "the place to talk about lovers, friends, and family," though it mostly seems to focus on that "lovers" part, relating to significant others—how to find them, keep them happy, keep yourself happy with them, and get the most out of your relationship. Lots of how-to columns and features help readers navigate everything from sex to weddings, with extensive resources and experts available, including a slot for guest experts.

E-mail for queries: Stacia Ragolia at rags@mail.ivillage.com.

[For full listing see Parent Soup on page 157.]

RockLove.com, http://www.rocklove.com

Tortured Artists Publications & Productions, 2240 Saint Francis Dr., Palo Alto, CA 94303. Tel.: (650) 812-0483, fax: (650) 494-6953. Lisa Vian, managing editor.

"RockLove.com is an Internet portal that uses music as its window to the Internet. RockLove.com also has a 200+ store e-mall." Established: 1995. Fifty percent freelance written. Circulation: 33,000. Pays on publication. Byline usually given. Buys all rights. "Accept simultaneous submissions, but again, we buy exclusive and all rights."

E-mail for submissions: s&l@rocklove.com.

Editorial Needs: Book excerpts, entertainment, interview, music, new product, technology. "Editorial content includes: live show coverage, in-depth band interviews, CD recommendations, book and video recommendations, industry news and events." Query with published clips. Word length for articles: CD, book, video recs—500; live shows—1000–1500; interview features–2500 and up.

Payment: $25–$350 (varies).

Photos/Art: "No story published without exclusive photography to RockLove.com, which can be arranged through home office to coincide with show, interview writer has been assigned. Photo payment—$50–$500 per event (all pix for bands on a live show bill, an entire interview photo shoot, etc. Requirements: identification of subjects. All rights purchased on photos."

Advice from Market: "The best way to learn to write for RockLove.com is to study the site thoroughly and read the passion and sense of fandom with which RockLove.com seeks to bring the fan more in touch with the subject being written about. RockLove looks for big, bombastic stories that go beyond the music, lifestories that will bring curious readers from around the globe to the site. However, we don't look to use the same subjects being offered up in large online and print publications. Also, RockLove.com loves to break new acts, as well as revisit established veterans."

Sacramento CitySearch, http://www.sacramento.citysearch.com
Ticketmaster Online CitySearch, 790 East Colorado Blvd., Suite 200, Pasadena, CA 91101. Tel.: (626) 405-0050, fax: (626) 405-9929. Michael Phillips, editor.
   [For full listing see Atlanta CitySearch on page 97.]

St. Louis CitySearch, http://www.stlouis.citysearch.com
Ticketmaster Online CitySearch, 790 East Colorado Blvd., Suite 200, Pasadena, CA 91101. Tel.: (626) 405-0050, fax: (626) 405-9929. Michael Phillips, editor.
   [For full listing see Atlanta CitySearch on page 97.]

Salon, http://www.salon.com
[See full listing on page 81 in "Top Ten Places to be Published Online."]

San Diego Sidewalk, http://www.sandiego.sidewalk.com
Microsoft, Mission Brewery Plaza, 2150 West Washington St., Suite 110, San Diego, CA 92110. Tel.: (619) 542-4300, fax: (619) 542-4399. Kristin Ewald, executive producer.
   "Guide to arts, entertainment, and shopping in San Diego." Peruse the site and query before submitting.
   E-mail for queries: Kristin Ewald, executive producer, at kristine@microsoft.com.
   [For full listing see New York Sidewalk listing on page 78.]

San Francisco Sidewalk, http://www.sanfrancisco.sidewalk.com
Microsoft, 585 Howard St., 3rd floor, San Francisco, CA 94105. Tel.: (415) 547-4300, fax: (415) 547-4343. Beth Cataldo, executive producer.
   "Guide to arts, entertainment, and shopping in San Francisco."
   Address for queries: Beth Cataldo doesn't accept e-mail queries; fax or mail queries with the contact information above.
   [For full listing see New York Sidewalk listing on page 78.]

San Jose CitySearch, http://www.sanjose.citysearch.com
Ticketmaster Online CitySearch, 790 East Colorado Blvd., Suite 200, Pasadena, CA 91101. Tel.: (626) 405-0050, fax: (626) 405-9929. Michael Phillips, editor.
[For full listing see Atlanta CitySearch on page 97.]

Seattle CitySearch, http://www.seattle.citysearch.com
Ticketmaster Online CitySearch, 790 East Colorado Blvd., Suite 200, Pasadena, CA 91101. Tel.: (626) 405-0050, fax: (626) 405-9929. Michael Phillips, editor.
[For full listing see Atlanta CitySearch on page 97.]

Seattle Sidewalk, http://www.seattle.sidewalk.com
Microsoft, 401 Second Ave. South, Suite 101, Court in the Square, Seattle, WA 98104. Tel.: (206) 621-5200, fax: (206) 621-5201. Jan Even, executive producer.
"Guide to arts, entertainment, and shopping in Seattle."
E-mail for queries: Jan Even at janeven@microsoft.com.
[For full listing see New York Sidewalk listing on page 78.]

Sfbg.com: the Web Site of the San Francisco Bay Guardian Newsweekly, http://www.sfbg.com
Bay Guardian Inc., 520 Hampshire, San Francisco, CA 94110. Tel.: (415) 255-3100, fax: (415) 255-8955. Bruce Brugmann, editor and publisher.
"Sfbg.com carries all the content from the print edition, in addition to a number of Web-exclusive columnists. Columns vary from news and advice to general interest and satire." Established 1995. Sixty percent freelance written. Circulation: 100,000. Pays on acceptance. Byline given. Buys varied rights. Reports in 1 week on queries; "depends" on manuscripts.
E-mail for queries: rob_neill@sfbg.com.
Editorial Needs: Entertainment, essays, exposé, humor, interview, music. Query with published clips.
Payment: $25–$100. Sometimes pays the expenses of writers on assignment.
Photos/Art: State availability of photos with submission. Negotiates

payment individually. Requires identification of subjects. Buys varied rights.

Advice from Market: "Generally, we employ columnists rather than one-off pieces. But I'll listen to any idea. Send queries to [Rob Neill, editor] at rob_neill@sfbg.com."

SiliconAlleyDaily.com, http://www.siliconalleydaily.com
Tel.: (212) 475-8000. Kirin Kalia, managing editor.

This is an offshoot service of the *Silicon Alley Reporter*, a New York City insider-type print publication on the local Internet economy, and its Web site. Peruse the site and query before submitting.

E-mail for queries: Kirin Kalia at kirin@siliconalleydaily.com.

Payment: $150 for reviews.

Advice from Writers: Writers confirm that SiliconAlleyDaily.com does pay for online freelance material, specifically reviews, at $150 each.

Singularities, http://www.wwco.com/scifi
Wizard Workshop and Company, 320 Woodmere Dr., Vinton, VA 24179. Danny Adams, editor.

This market describes itself as "science fiction, fantasy, and horror for those interested in something a little different." Established August 1996. One hundred percent freelance written. Circulation: 3,000. Pays on publication. Byline given. Buys first electronic rights. Accepts simultaneous and previously published submissions. Reports in 1 week on queries, 4–6 weeks on manuscripts.

E-mail for for queries and questions (not submissions): dda@ wwco.com.

Editorial Needs: Entertainment, essays, fiction, interviews, poetry, technology. Send complete manuscript. Word length for articles: 500–15,000.

Payment: $25 and up, for assigned articles; $5–½ cent/word up to $75 for unsolicited articles.

Photos/Art: Send photos with submission. Negotiates payment individually. Requires captions, model releases, identification of subjects. Buys onetime rights.

Advice from Market: "Please follow the guidelines given by the [online] magazine (sounds like common sense, but it doesn't always happen). . . . and please no excessive sex or violence unless it's absolutely integral to the storyline. You don't need to summarize the story in the cover letter; just tell me about yourself and let the story do the rest of the work."

Slate, http://www.slate.com
Microsoft, 1 Microsoft Way, Redmond, WA 98052. Tel.: (425) 882-8080. Michael Kinsley, editor.

Slate is high-profile, literary, and lucrative for freelancers, covering genres from poetry to politics, news to celebrity noise, all with the authority and panache you'd expect from editor Michael Kinsley and the clout you'd expect from Microsoft's deep pockets. Peruse the site and query before submitting.

E-mail for queries: letters@slate.com is monitored for queries, according to an assistant in the editorial department.

Slaughterhouse, http://www.slaughterhouse.com
Andover Advanced Technologies, 50 Nagog Park Rd., 2nd floor, Acton, MA 01720. Tel.: (978) 635-5300, fax: (978) 635-5326. Robin Miller, senior editor.

The folks at Slaughterhouse focus their content on technology news and current information as well as reviews of the latest software. They also provide downloads to most current Internet tools, media plug-ins, and games.

[For full listing see AndoverNews on page 94.]

Snap.com, http://www.snap.com
Tel.: (415) 875-7900. Deanna Dawson, managing producer.

Snap.com is a portal or a hub or a search engine with many links to many things. In fact, links to all things from crime-fighting resources to computer games. Deanna Dawson explained Snap.com's freelance process: "We hire writers to write up specific assignments for us and do not publish or accept submissions. Our writers only write small two-line reviews for Web sites." Peruse the site and query before submitting.

E-mail for queries/resumes: Deanna Dawson at deannad@ snap.com.

Advice from Writers: One writer from NWU's database gave up rights as "work-made-for-hire" for $100. The writer stressed that the "editor could not negotiate anything—good editor, no power." The writer also noted, "Several times payment was 60-plus days late (the last invoice still [had] not been paid after 90 days)." [Please note that this writer's comments were not referring to this listing's contact, Deanna Dawson.]

SonicNet: Music News of the World, http://www.sonicnet.com
SonicNet, Inc., 375 Alabama St., Suite 480, San Francisco, CA 94110. Please do not call or fax. Michael Goldberg, SonicNet editorial director/Addicted To Noise editor in chief.

"SonicNet Music News of the World is a daily music news area that is updated all day long. We publish about 20 pieces of original editorial content per weekday in the news area. Twenty percent of our daily music news (http://www.sonicnet.com/news) is written by freelance writers." Established December 1994. Circulation: withheld. "Portions of our editorial content reach tens of millions of music fans each month. We provide headline music news to The Box music television channel, which can be accessed in over 30 million homes. Radio and print media also make use of some of our content. Portions of our content also appear on third-party Web sites in the U.S. and abroad." Pays on publication—currently checks go out 4 to 6 weeks after publication. Byline given. Buys all rights in all media. "We are only interested in original material that has never been published before, and it must conform to our very specific, [high] standards." On queries and manuscripts: "If we're interested, you'll hear from us. If not, you won't."

E-mail for queries: Lisa@sonicnet.com.

Editorial Needs: Music, news. Short "Scan" items (three sentences—50–75 words), longer news pieces range from 400–800 words.

Payment: Negotiates payment individually. Minimal expenses covered on occasion.

Photos/Art: State availability of photos with submission. Negotiates payment individually. Buys all online rights.

Advice from Market: "Study our music news, album reviews, and

Addicted to Noise interviews and features. We are looking for writers who can deliver the kind of editorial that you will find in abundance on the Web sites."

Spaceways Weekly: The Canadian E-mail Magazine of Science Fiction and Fantasy, http://spaceways.mirror.org
London Application Solutions, Inc., 148 York St., London, Ontario N6A 1A9, Canada. Rigel D. Chiokis, editor.

"We focus on science fiction and fantasy short stories which have an upbeat ending and/or positive theme to them. No gratuitous violence, sex, sexism, etc. We do not accept pieces which promote hate, intolerance, segregation, etc. We do not accept historical fiction or religious fiction. Our readers are adults from various walks of life, including many SF & F writers." Established September 1997. One hundred percent freelance written. Circulation: 100+ subscribers. Pays on acceptance. Byline given. Buys first world electronic rights. Accepts simultaneous and previously published submissions. Reports in 3 weeks on queries, 3–6 weeks on manuscripts.

E-mail for submissions: spaceways@mirror.org.

Editorial Needs: Fiction. Send complete manuscript. Word length for stories: 1000–5000.

Payment: 1 cent/word (Canadian funds).

Advice from Market: "Visit http://spaceways.mirror.org and check the Writers' Info area. Visit http://www.speculations.com/rumormill and read through the postings there, especially the I Wish Writers Wouldn't topic. The worst mistake a freelancer can make is to ignore the guidelines. The guidelines are to tell you how to send stuff to an editor. Ignore them at your own peril. Visit our Web site to read our guidelines at http://spaceways.mirror.org/guide.html."

SportsJones Magazine: The Online Magazine for Sports, http://www.sportsjones.com
SportsJones.com, Inc., 965 Harpeth Bend Dr., Nashville, TN 37221. Jeff Merron, executive editor.

"SportsJones is a daily online sports magazine featuring alternative coverage of all sports. Our focus is on great writing for a worldwide audience." This book's senior contributing writer Karen Morrissey affirms, "Sportsjones.com is sports lovers writing about the heart and soul of sports and the athletes who play them." Established June 1998. Fifty percent freelance written. Circulation: withheld. Pays on publication. Byline given. Buys all rights. Reports in 2 weeks on queries; 1 month on manuscripts.

E-mail for queries: sjeditor@sportsjones.com.

Editorial Needs: Book excerpts, essays, exposé, health/fitness, interview, opinion, personal experience, technology, travel, sports, women's. Query. Word length for articles: 500–2000.

Payment: $25–$300; payment for unsolicited articles $100–$300.

Photos/Art: Freelancers should state availability of photos with submission. Negotiates payment individually. Requires captions and identification of subjects.

Advice from Market: "SportsJones is a general-interest sport Web site with room for a wide variety of viewpoints. Writers should be thoroughly familiar with our site and with the SportsJones style before submitting stories. All stories should be written with an international audience in mind."

Stocktalker, http://www.stocktalker.com

As cited at WritersMarkets.com: The FREE, marketing e-mag for professional writers and journalists, "Stocktalker has actively searched for freelance writers. Column topics include reports on particular stocks or industries, reports on market activity and market news, and trading strategies." Peruse the site and query before submitting.

E-mail for queries: editorial@stocktalker.com.

Suck, http://www.suck.com

Wired Ventures, 660 Third St., San Francisco, CA 94107. Tel.: (415) 276-8788, fax: (415) 276-8499. Tim Cavanaugh, editor.

Confirm contact. "Suck specializes in detonating media myths. The journalistic equivalent of running with scissors, Suck's daily posts are too literate to be called rants, too obsessed with popular culture to be considered academic and too funny to be taken seriously. We are not afraid to take on easy targets: public television, Anthony Robbins, Canada, cyberdelia, Tiger Woods. Our readers are probably smarter than we are but we try not make them feel bad about it—they look to us for cheap laughs and juvenile finger pointing. We rarely disappoint." Established August 1995. Sixty-five to 70 percent freelance written. Circulation: 190,000. Pays on publication. Byline not given. "Most Suck contributors prefer to remain anonymous. (Would you want your parents to know you wrote for 'Suck'?) All bylines are pseudonyms, but every author gets a bio page where he/she may reveal his/her 'true' identity. Why they'd want to is, of course, a mystery." Buys exclusive rights for 60 days, shared after that. Editorial lead time is 2 days. Accepts simultaneous submissions. Reports in a couple of weeks at the very longest, usually within a couple of days on queries and manuscripts.

E-mail for queries: sucksters@suck.com.

Editorial Needs: Nonfiction: humor, personal experience, essays, exposé, historical/nostalgic, opinion. "We don't want anything about: how Microsoft is evil, how the Web sucks, why advertising is bad or what's wrong with newbies on the Net. No Web site reviews. No music reviews. Don't use the word 'suck' in a clever pun." Send complete manuscript. Word length: 600–1200.

Payment: Pays $600 for assigned articles, $450 for unsolicited articles. Sometimes pays expenses of writers on assignment.

Advice from Market: "Submit via e-mail, put the essay in the body of the message [and] that it is a submission in the subject line. Include a phone number and e-mail address where you can reliably be reached. Don't worry about including clever links and don't worry about submitting it with HTML tags. Unadorned insight will be impressive enough. A chimp can put it into HTML format and his brother could find links. If you have a chimp available for these duties, of course, let us know." At press time for this book, Suck isn't open to new freelance submissions. See www.marketsforwriters.com for any status update, or peruse the site and query before submitting.

Advice from Writers: A writer from NWU's database reported payments of $450–$500 for 650–1000 words, and $100 for 150-word short news. The writer reported selling "All rights exclusive for 60 days" and cited Suck as not willing to negotiate.

Suite101.com: Real People Helping Real People, http://www.suite101.com

Suite101.com, Inc., 390-1122 Mainland St., Vancouver, BC V6B 5L1, Canada. Tel.: (604) 682-1400, fax: (604) 682-3277. Jason Pamer, editor in chief.

This market describes itself as "an online best-of-Web guide that provides an efficient means of locating quality content on the Web. The average Suite101.com user is highly educated; average age is 37; 60 percent female, 40 percent male." Established June 1996. One hundred percent freelance written. Circulation: withheld. Pays on acceptance. Byline given. Buys 90-day exclusive rights.

E-mail for information: jason@suite101.com. ("Submissions all made [via] the Web site.")

Editorial Needs: Health/fitness, how-to, humor, general interest, historical, inspirational, men's, music, opinion, personal experience, poetry, religious, technical, technology, teen, trade, travel, sports, women's. Query. Word length for articles: 300–1000.

Payment: "Payments made to editors are not based on a per-article scale. Instead, it's an honorarium to help pay for time spent online doing Suite101.com-related work. Suite101.com contributing editors do more than submit articles, they also review Web sites and participate in online discussions. Editors who submit weekly articles receive $25 a month. Editors who submit biweekly articles receive $20 a month and editors who submit monthly articles receive $15 a month."

Photos/Art: No additional payment. Buys onetime rights.

Advice from Market: See http://www.suite101.com/editorapp/ member.cfm.

Advice from Writers: One contributing editor described Suite101 .com as "a scaled-down version of About.com," and went on to say that the "lousy pay (just $25 per month for a weekly story and links)" was balanced out by having "a lot more freedom and less aggravation than at About.com."

Surfer Magazine, http://www.surfermag.com
Emap Petersen, P.O. Box 1028, Dana Point, CA 92629. Tel.: (949) 496-5922, fax: (949) 496-7849. Scott Bass, online editor.

This market describes itself as "hardcore surfing." Less than 5 percent freelance written. Circulation: 130,000. "We'll call you about payment." Byline given. Reports in "2 weeks to never" on queries and [not at all] on manuscripts."

E-mail for queries: surfermag@surfermag.com

Editorial Needs: Exposé, health/fitness, how-to, humor, fiction, general interest, historical, new product, technical, technology, women's. Query with published clips. Word length for articles: 400–1000.

Payment: "Varies." Sometimes pays the expenses of writers on assignment.

Photos/Art: State availability of photos with query and then send photos with submission. No additional payment. Requires captions, model releases, and identification of subjects. Buys all rights.

Advice from Market: "We are busy. If you're not professional, don't bother. If you are professional, it better be good. More often than not, we glance over queries and throw them. It better be unique."

Swoon, http://www.swoon.com
CondéNet, 140 East 45th St., 37th floor, New York, NY 10017. (Note: as of press time, CondéNet may be moving to 342 Madison Ave. Be sure to confirm address.) Tel.: (212) 880-2196, fax: (212) 880-8121. Melissa Weiner, editor in chief. (See page 46 for interview with Melissa Weiner.)

"Swoon is the online hotspot for all things dating, mating, and relating for men and women in their twenties and thirties." Established July 1996. Twenty-five percent freelance written. Circulation: 700,000. Pays on acceptance. Byline given, but sometimes under a pseudonym. Buys all rights. "We only contact people if we are interested in their submissions. Time varies."

E-mail for queries: swoonfeedback@swoon.com.

Editorial Needs: "Currently Swoon has freelance columnists that fulfill our astrological, relationship, celebrity, and musical needs. They may expand in the future, but those are the areas we freelance out." Query with published clips. Word length for articles: 250–500.

Payment: Varies. "We don't pay by the word." Sometimes pays the expenses of writers on assignment.

Tampa Bay CitySearch, http://www.tampabay.citysearch.com
Ticketmaster Online CitySearch, 790 East Colorado Blvd., Suite 200,

Pasadena, CA 91101. Tel.: (626) 405-0050, fax: (626) 405-9929. Michael Phillips, editor.

[For full listing see Atlanta CitySearch on page 97.]

TechSightings, http://www.techsightings.com
Andover Advanced Technologies, 50 Nagog Park Rd., 2nd floor, Acton, MA 01720. Tel.: (978) 635-5300, fax: (978) 635-5326. Robin Miller, senior editor.

TechSightings is made up of "Daily Reviews of the Best High-Tech Sights on the Net!" Column topics range from Web building tools and bandwidth issues to the latest hardware glitches and career commentary on the Internet.

[For full listing see AndoverNews on page 94.]

Terrace Times, The, http://www.windowbox.com
The Balcony Gardener, Inc., 614 San Vicente Blvd., Suite G, Santa Monica, CA 90402. Tel.: (888) GARDEN-B, fax: (310) 394-0636. Ann Cherin, information manager.

"The Terrace Times is a monthly online magazine with a 'what's new' section that features seasonal articles related to container gardening. Our audience is primarily inexperienced gardeners from urban and suburban areas, with limited time/space for or interest in intense backyard gardening." Established May 1999. Ninety percent freelance written. Circulation: 5000. Pays on acceptance. Byline given. Buys all rights. "I usually get back to writers within 24 hrs . . . a couple of days at most if I get busy."

E-mail for queries: Ann@windowbox.com.

Editorial Needs: Entertainment, how-to, humor, fiction, historical, new product, personal experience, poetry. "Note: all must relate to container gardening." Query. Word length for articles: 200–400.

Payment: $10.

Photos/Art: State availability of photos with submission. Negotiates payment individually. Buys negotiable rights.

Advice from Market: "We don't currently have our guidelines online. Writers should get in touch with Ann Cherin by e-mail (Ann@windowbox.com) with their ideas for topics and a writing sample. Ann works with each writer individually to figure out timelines and content. Writers should spend some time reading existing articles at Windowbox.com to get a feel for the lighthearted, straightforward style of the site. All of the articles are concise and 'scannable' for Web users who tend to scan rather than read. So we do not accept articles longer than 500 words, and prefer short paragraphs. We reserve the right to edit any article as needed to fit the format of our site."

TheKnot.com, http://www.theknot.com
Alison Salat, managing producer.

TheKnot.com bills itself as "The #1 wedding Web site and registry." Content spans from Planning Advice and Fashion to Honeymoon Escapes. This market didn't complete our questionnaire, but writers report that it pays for online freelance material. Peruse the site and query before submitting.

E-mail for queries: Alison Salat at alison@theknot.com.

Through Darkling Glass, http://www.dynamics.mb.ca/glass
Through Darkling Glass, 15 Hardy Bay, Winnipeg, Manitoba R2M 5M5, Canada. Robyn Enns, executive editor.

"Glass is intended to showcase the best of the science fiction and high fantasy genre; we look for quality far above quantity. We would prefer not to publish at all rather than take whatever comes our way. Our audience is age 15 and up." Established June 1997. Ninety-five to 100 percent freelance written. Circulation: 150 readers per month. Pays on acceptance. Byline given. Buys first electronic publishing rights (copyright reverts back to author two months after publication). Accepts simultaneous and previously published submissions. Reports in 1 week on queries, 2 weeks on manuscripts.

E-mail for queries: gryffin@mailexcite.com.

Editorial Needs: [fiction] writing for the sf/fantasy genre. Query. Word length for stories: 2500, but not firm.

Payment: $5–$10.

Photos/Art: State availability of photos with submission. Pays $5–$10. Buys onetime rights.

Advice from Market: "No fairy tales, moral of the story, etc. This zine is intended for an adult audience. Do not follow usual stereotypes as regards character (e.g., white horned horse that cleans streams being the extent of 'culture' for unicorns). Destroy stereotypes. There is a *lot* of fantasy out there—give your piece a unique slant on what may seem to be an overused topic. Read the zine, in particular Joe Murphy and Robyn Enns for content as well as execution, and Lida Broadhurst for execution. There are two points I consider as editor: strong character development—an identifiable 'voice' instead of a generic narration, highly developed culture/background that places these characters in a strong future or medieval-style setting. Urban fantasy will also be accepted if it is exceptional/unique in execution. In other words, not a work of general fiction with a dragon thrown in. All pieces that create an in-depth culture for nonhuman characters are especially sought after. (Note: this does not mean talking unicorns. For an excellent example read *Watership Down* by Robert Adams.) Plot—fantasy or science fiction elements must be integral to the story. This must be evident by the end of the first page. Magic is not necessary (in fact, is not preferred as a central theme), but the genre should still be evident. The only things I will turn down at first glance are those with an occult or graphically sexual theme. Any questions can be directed to gryffin@mailexcite.com."

TIME Digital, http://www.timedigital.com
This book's senior contributing writer Karen Morrissey explains that "according to TIME Digital, 'whether you're an English major with a taste for gadgets or an information technology professional, TIME Digital Online is your daily source for smart jargon-free tech news.' Content features columns, real-time tech bargains, a supplementary newswire, and a discussion forum." Peruse the site and query before submitting.
   E-mail for queries: Nathaniel Wice at nwice@pathfinder.com.

Travel Channel: IVillage, http://www.ivillage.com/travel
iVillage: The Women's Network, 170 Fifth Ave., New York, NY 10010. Fax: (212) 604-9133. Kellie Krumplitsch, editorial director.
   IVillage's Travel channel takes an eclectic approach to transportation and vacations. Columns and features range from trip tips, travel

astrology, and travelers' journals to the more mainstream mantras of booking flights and renting cars.

E-mail for queries: Susan Weaver at sweaver@mail.ivillage.com.

[For full listing see Parent Soup on page 157.]

Travel-Watch, http://www.travel-watch.com
Craig Menefee, executive editor.

This market explains itself as "Featuring Online News, Features, Reviews & Profiles for Food, Wine, & Travel, Water & Snow Sports, & Entertainment." This market didn't complete our questionnaire, but writers report that it pays for online freelance material. Peruse the site and query before submitting.

E-mail for queries: Craig Menefee at cmenefee@travel-watch.com.

Triangle CitySearch, The, http://www.triangle.citysearch.com
Ticketmaster Online CitySearch, 790 East Colorado Blvd., Suite 200, Pasadena, CA 91101. Tel.: (626) 405-0050, fax: (626) 405-9929. ["The Triangle" refers to the North Carolina area.] The Triangle office tel.: (919) 549-0100. Michael Phillips, editor.

[For full listing see Atlanta CitySearch on page 97.]

Trip.com Newsstand Section, http://www.trip.com/completetraveler
TheTrip.com, 6436 S. Racine Circle, Englewood, CO 80111. Tel.: (303) 708-7224, fax: (303) 790-9350. Gil Asakawa, content producer potentate.

"TRIP.com's Newsstand content primarily addresses travel and travel-related issues of business travelers, with feature stories, columnists, and user-content message boards." Established September 1996. Ninety percent freelance written. Circulation: withheld. Pays on publication. Byline given. Buys online and offline (negotiable) rights.

E-mail for queries: gil@TRIP.com (or editor@TRIP.com).

Editorial Needs: Business travel. Query with published clips. Word length for articles: 800.

Payment: "Varies—negotiable."

Advice from Market: "Cannot use and am not interested in destination 'travelogue' style stories; prefer creative approaches to covering business-travel-related issues."

Tripod, http://www.tripod.com
Bet Alwin, editorial director.

Tripod is part of the Lycos network. Bet Alwin says, as this book goes to press, that she does not want to encourage multiple inquiries from freelance writers. She explains, "We're pulling way back on the amount of external content we purchase for the Tripod site, favoring developing a strategy of content integration among the Lycos network sites. Our content focus, too, has changed. Where once we were positioned as an online lifestyles zine with related community features content, we are honing our content focus to home page–building advice and tips and online e-commerce (which is the focus of our business)." Peruse the site and query before submitting.

E-mail for queries: Bet Alwin at balwin@tripod.com.

Twin Cities Sidewalk, http://www.twincities.sidewalk.com
Microsoft, Colwell Building, 123 N. Third St., Suite 605, Minneapolis, MN 55401. Tel.: (612) 204-3800, fax: (612) 204-3801. Chris Boone, executive producer.

"Guide to arts, entertainment and shopping in the Twin Cities." Established May 1997. Eighty-five percent freelance written. Circulation: withheld. Pays on acceptance. Byline given. Buys all rights. Editorial lead time: 2–3 weeks. Accepts simultaneous submissions. Reports in 1 week on queries and manuscripts. This market didn't complete our questionnaire, but we're assuming its pay and policies are the same as New York Sidewalk (see page 78), its sister publication in Microsoft's Sidewalk network. Peruse the site and query before submitting.

E-Mail for queries: Chris Boone at cboone@microsoft.com.

Editorial Needs: Reviews/previews of events. Query with published clips. Word length for articles: 25–100. Columns, 75–200.

Payment: "Pays a flat weekly rate for contributors." Sometimes pays expenses of writers on assignment.

Photos/Art: Send photos with submission. Reviews contact sheets, transparencies, prints. Negotiates payment individually. Captions, model releases, identification of subjects required. Buys all, universal rights.

USATODAY.com, http://www.usatoday.com
Tel.: (703) 276-3400. Jim Schulte, editor in chief.

USATODAY.com does buy freelance writing, but not much. In fact, " 'Very few' [pieces] would be an overstatement," according to Chris Fruitrich, deputy editor at USATODAY.com. "We will on occasion go out seeking someone to write on a specific topic, but we concentrate our efforts on breaking news and do not have the time to sift through unsolicited pieces." He will accept "resumes and limited clips" to cfruitrich@usatoday.com, but wants it to be very clear that freelance writers shouldn't call or follow up. "We'll call you when we need something. I don't mean to sound sour about this, but we really spend 99 percent of our energy on breaking news and its associated elements." Peruse the site before sending resume and clips.

E-mail for queries: Chris Fruitrich at cfruitrich@usatoday.com. (See above caveats.)

Utah CitySearch, http://www.utah.citysearch.com
Ticketmaster Online CitySearch, 790 East Colorado Blvd., Suite 200, Pasadena, CA 91101. Tel.: (626) 405-0050, fax: (626) 405-9929. Utah office tel.: (801) 994-4500. Michael Phillips, editor.

[For full listing see Atlanta CitySearch on page 97.]

Victoria Brooks' Greatest Escapes Travel Webzine,
http://www.greatestescapes.com
GreatestEscapes.com, Inc., 5255 Gulf Pl., West Vancouver, BC V7W 2V9, Canada. Victoria Brooks, editor in chief.

"Our Web zine at www.greatestescapes.com provides readers with authoritative and helpful coverage of travel destinations through creatively written stories that include well-researched practical information. Our audience consists primarily of sophisticated travelers who want their travels and adventures to be memorable experiences." Established February 1998.

E-mail for queries: editor@greatestescapes.com.
Payment: "We will be paying $75–$100 for articles 750–1200 words."
Advice from Market: "Full writing guidelines [and payment rates] are posted on the Web site."

Virtuabooks Publishing, http://www.virtuabooks.com
Virtuabooks Publishing, 4305 State Bridge Rd., PMB 231, Suite 103, Alpharetta, GA 30022. Tel.: (404) 456-1033, fax: (770) 569-8143. Robert E. Gelinas, editor.

"We publish mass-market commercial fiction (no nonfiction) as virtual books, or e-books. They are full-length literary works, purchased and downloaded via the Internet for immediate enjoyment. Our target audience consists of business travelers with laptops (who don't wish to carry more than they have to in their briefcases), office workers, children, and home users." Established March 1999. One hundred percent freelance written. Circulation: not available yet. "We pay monthly on actual number of books sold. Our royalty model is described in detail on our Web site on the Authors page." Byline given. Buys electronic, hard copy (hardcover and paperback), and audio. Accepts simultaneous and previously published submissions (if all rights are reverted). "Queries aren't required, but working through an established literary agent is. Responds to manuscripts usually within 30 days."

E-mail address for editorial submissions: eic@virtuabooks.com.

Editorial Needs: Entertainment, humor, fiction, historical. "Send complete manuscript via literary agent. Actually, our complete book proposal guidelines are spelled out on the Agent page of our Web site." Word length for articles: 30,000–no maximum.

Payment: "Our royalty model pays the author $1 per copy sold, as well as paying his or her literary agent a full commission against royalties, so the author nets a full $1."

Advice from Market: "Go to www.virtuabooks.com. There you will find complete pages for Authors, Agents, About Virtuabooks, and our FAQ page. All of these will tell you everything you need to know about Virtuabooks Publishing and how to submit material for publication."

Wall Street Journal Interactive Edition, The, Interactive Journal, http://wsj.com
[See full listing on page 83 in "Top Ten Places to be Published Online."]

Washington, D.C. Sidewalk, http://www.washington.sidewalk.com
Microsoft, 1818 N St., Suite 300, Washington, DC 20036.

Tel.: (202) 721-1900, fax: (202) 872-0139. Gina Bittner, executive producer.

"Guide to arts, entertainment, and shopping in Washington, D.C." Peruse the site and query before submitting.

E-mail for queries: Gina Bittner at gbittner@microsoft.com.

[For full listing see New York Sidewalk listing on page 78.]

Webdeveloper.com, http://www.webdeveloper.com
David Fiedler, editor in chief.

Webdeveloper.com, part of the Internet.com network, lives up to all the techie mystique of its moniker. From "JavaScript 'Zip Code Validation' " to "Putting a database on the Web," this site offers seasoned developers every topic and tutorial they need to create Web sites that work better. Peruse the site and query before submitting.

E-mail for queries: David Fiedler at dfiedler@internet.com or david@internet.com.

Web Digest for Marketers, http://wdfm.com.
This market didn't complete our questionnaire, but it occasionally looks for freelance writers. When the need arises, its editorial request reads: "Looking for one (and possibly 2) freelance writers who would primarily write 100–120 word reviews for this fortnightly e-mail newsletter which plans on going weekly soon. This person or people would be referred to as a 'WDFM co-editor.' A co-editor is responsible for producing an entire issue, which typically runs between 15 and 21 reviews. The 'freelance availability' is immediate and ongoing. WDFM is a free service that is read by over 60,000 people monthly. A solid writing and marketing background is most definitely preferred for this position."

E-mail for editorial resumes: "Interested parties can send resumes to freelance@wdfm.com and sample the newsletter itself at wdfm.com."

Payment: "Remuneration is commensurate with this marketplace."

Advice from Market: "I don't want to receive solicitations for columnists or freelancers who wish to write articles. Once in a very great while, I look for an editor. It is only then that I look for appropriate writers with marketing and Internet backrounds. These are short reviews, no more than 120 words. One editor handles the entire issue. If you wish to reflect this information in your book about WDFM, that would be great and appreciated . . . but please, make it so I don't receive requests for freelance articles on an ongoing basis. I get way too many of those as is. It never ceases to astonish me that people will submit samples without reviewing the content and nature of the publication first. I know they want to get many queries in, but being a former freelance writer myself, and still a columnist, I've learned from experience that it is much better to pitch only a few publications with some well-targeted, thoughtful, on-topic ideas or formats than to approach with a one-size-fits-all strategy. I've been the pitchee and the pitcher. The more focused, the more apt I am to pay attention. I don't wish to appear crappy about it, merely clear so that it works in the best interest of both writer and publisher."

Webmonkey, http://www.webmonkey.com
Wired Digital, 660 3rd St., 4th floor, San Francisco, CA 94107. Tel.: (415) 276-8400. Kristin Windbigler, editorial producer. Phillip Bailey, executive assistant for content and design.

This site is a "how-to guide for Web developers," covering everything from mastering Java to building your own computer from scratch. There also a section called "Webmonkey for kids: Lessons and projects for the next generation of Web builders." This market didn't complete our questionnaire, but it confirmed that it buys online freelance material. Peruse the site and query before submitting.

E-mail for queries: Kristin Windbigler at kristin@wired.com or Phillip Bailey at phil@wired.com.

Windows Magazine, http://www.winmag.com
Mike Elgan, editor.

The crux of Windows Magazine is in its own tag: "PC Tips, News and Reviews." Columns and features show readers how to make the most of their PC—software, hardware, new releases, glitch fixes, and a community of PC comrades expounding on the virtues and vices of their Windows experiences. Peruse the site and query before submitting.

E-mail for queries: Mike Elgan at melgan@winmag.com.

Wine Spectator Online, http://www.winespectator.com
Dana Nigro, news editor.

"Wine Spectator Online is written 'for people serious about wine'—but who don't take themselves or their wines too seriously. We think our readers want to know the stories behind the wines that are well known, well respected, and worth their attention." Pays on publication. Byline given. Buys global publication rights—exclusive rights for magazine and Web site and right to anthologize/archive. "Usually [reports] within a matter of days on a query if interested; solicited manuscripts are quickly edited.

E-mail for queries: Dana Nigro at dnigro@mshanken.com. "E-mail query, with explanation of wine-and-food background."

Editorial Needs: "We are interested in short news stories about the world of wine. Length can vary from 50–500 words, but the material must be timely and concisely written. Again, wine-related and high-end-restaurant-related news only."

Payment: "Varies. Timely news stories of 50–500 words are paid at $25–$150, depending on length and importance." Word length for articles: 75–500. Sometimes pays the expenses of writers on assignment.

Photos/Art: Freelancers should state availability of photos with submission. Negotiates payment individually. Requires identification of subjects.

Advice from Market: "Extremely limited number of submissions accepted. No unsolicited material. Must have prior experience writing about wine or food, or demonstrate extensive knowledge of the subject matter. No articles from people currently employed by wineries or wine-related companies. Wine or restaurant news should be of interest to high-end, national U.S. audience. Must be able to work on very short deadlines."

Wired News, http://www.wirednews.com
Wired Digital, 660 3rd St., 4th floor, San Francisco, CA 94107. Tel.: (415) 276-8400. Alison Macondray, managing editor.

Wired News features Net-savvy reports across business, culture, technology, and politics. This market didn't complete our questionnaire, but it confirmed that it buys online freelance material. Peruse the site and query before submitting.

E-mail for queries: Alison Macondray at alison@wired.com.

Women.com, http://www.women.com
[See full listing on page 84 in "Top Ten Places to be Published Online."]

Word, http://www.word.com
[See full listing on page 85 in "Top Ten Places to be Published Online."]

Write Markets Report, The: The Only Source of Markets Needing Writers Today, http://www.writersmarkets.com
Deep South Publishing Company, P.O. Box 912, Andover, MA 01810. (Note: moving at press time. Confirm address.) Angela Adair-Hoy, publisher.

"Each issue features 50+ paying markets for writers, including each editor's current needs, along with feature articles on how to make more money writing." Established June 1997. Twenty percent freelance written. Circulation: 28,000. Pays on acceptance. Byline given. Buys first electronic rights. Accepts previously published submissions. Reports in 1–2 days on queries.

E-mail for queries (doesn't accept unsolicited manuscripts): aadair@writersmarkets.com.

Editorial Needs: How-to, nonfiction, articles that teach writers how to make more money writing, including new venues for manuscript sales, marketing techniques, and secrets of successful freelancers. Query. Word length for articles: 600 maximum.

Payment: Flat fee of $50. Pays the expenses of writers on assignment.

Advice from Market: "If you have an idea that will help our readers increase their freelance income, please query us! See our detailed guidelines online at: www.writersmarkets.com/index-markets.htm.

Writer Online, http://www.novalearn.com/wol
Novation Learning Systems, Inc., 190 Mt. Vernon Ave., Rochester, NY 14620. Tel.: (716) 271-2250, fax: (716) 271-5602. Terry Boothman, publisher.

This market describes itself as "an electronic magazine and resource center for writers of all kinds, fiction, nonfiction, technical, and business." Established April 1998. Fifty percent freelance written. Circulation: 24,000 subscribers. Pays on publication. Byline given. Buys onetime, nonexclusive publishing rights, archival rights. Accepts simultaneous and previously published submissions. Reports in 1 month on queries, 1 to 2 months on manuscripts.

E-mail for submissions: manager@novalearn.com.

Editorial Needs: Book excerpts, entertainment, essays, how-to, humor, interview, opinion, personal experience, technical, trade. "Subject matter must be relevant to professional or aspiring writers." Query or send complete manuscript. Word length for articles: 800–1800.

Payment: $20–$100.

Photos/Art: State availability of photos with submission. No additional payment. "We are an electronic magazine and would expect electronic images." Requires captions. Buys onetime rights.

Advice from Market: "Writers' guidelines are available at the Web site, www.novalearn.com/wol, or by sending an e-mail to writers@ novalearn.com. We do not accept unsolicited fiction or poetry. Articles should be current, well-written, and relevant to the craft or marketing of writing: fiction, nonfiction, essay, technical, or business writing. Writers are advised to carefully read current and archived articles for a sense of our style and content.

Writersmarkets.com: The Free Marketing E-mag for Writers, http://www.writersmarkets.com
Deep South Publishing Company, P.O. Box 912, Andover, MA 01810. (Note: moving at press time. Confirm address.) Angela Adair-Hoy, publisher.

"Each issue features: free magazine offers for writers, links to guidelines available by e-mail, links to guidelines available online, current listings of paying markets for writers, and articles on how to make more money writing." Established June 1997. Thirty percent freelance written. Circulation: "distributed to 14,000+ writers on a biweekly basis by e-mail." Pays on publication. Byline given. "Sometimes (very generous bylines given)." Buys first electronic rights. Accepts previously published submissions. Reports in 1–2 days on queries.

E-mail for queries (doesn't accept unsolicited manuscripts): aadair@writersmarkets.com.

Editorial Needs: Book excerpts, how-to, inspirational, personal experience. "We really like articles that show what successful writers have done to increase their incomes; success stories; interviews; you-can-do-it-too articles." Query. Word length for articles: 300 maximum.

Payment: Flat fee of $10. Sometimes pays the expenses of writers on assignment.

Advice from Market: "If you are or know of a successful freelancer who wants to share their secrets, please query us! See our detailed guidelines online at: www.writersmarkets.com/index-markets.htm."

Writing for Dollars!, http://www.awoc.com/wfd
AWOC.COM, PMB 225, 2436 S I-35E, Suite 376, Denton, TX 76205. Dan Case, editor.

"Writing for Dollars! is a free, monthly newsletter for writers who want to start selling their work or to increase their present writing income. How to sell to specific markets, interviews with successful writers, and new ways to make money as a writer are some of the themes in each issue. WFD is distributed by e-mail. Back issues can be found at http://www.awoc.com/wfd.cfm." Established December 1997. Ninety-five percent freelance written. Circulation: 11,000. Pays on acceptance. Byline given. Buys exclusive first-use onetime rights in the e-mailed newsletter, Writing for Dollars!, after which Awoc.com retains the nonexclusive right to archive and display the article online on its Web site. Reports in 7 days by e-mail, 6 weeks by snail mail on queries and manuscripts.

E-mail for queries: editor@awoc.com.

Editorial Needs: Book excerpts, how-to, interview. Query. Word length for articles: 500–1000.

Payment: $15.

Advice from Market: "To subscribe for free, send the message SUBSCRIBE to: wfd-request@MailingList.net. Contact editor@awoc .com for our writers' guidelines by e-mail. We prefer to be queried by e-mail. Read a few back issues at www.awoc.com/wfd.cfm and the writers' guidelines before you query. We rarely buy unsolicited manuscripts. Do yourself a favor and query us with your idea before you write the article. We can help you get the right slant. We don't do articles on 'How to Overcome Writer's Block,' or 'How I Got Shafted by XYZ Magazine.' The most common reasons for rejection is 'not the right subject or slant' and 'not the correct number of words' (500–1000)."

Web Writing Resources
Recommended by Online Editors

Bartlett's Familiar Quotations, http://www.columbia.edu/acis/bartleby/
bartlett/.—Noah Robischon, editor of now-defunct Netley News (see
interview, page 48)

Blip, The, http://www.theblip.com. "A great place to unwind. Their games
are a lot of fun."—Alice Bradley (see interview, page 43), Charged (see listing, page 107)

Bookwire, http://www.bookwire.com.—Ellen Ullman (see interview, page
48), Princeton Review Online (see listing, page 161)

Feed, http://www.feedmag.com. "Solid critical writing, with intriguing use of
Webbified annotation."—Marisa Bowe (see interview, page 46), Word (see
listing, page 85). "One of the three best sites in terms of content. Feed also
does the best job of integrating their Feedbag discussions and linking to
sites outside theirs; they make the most of the community aspect of the
Web."—Alice Bradley, Charged

Great Dog Breed Pages, http://www.dogpatch.org/breed.html. "My time
waster/vice site."—Ellen Ullman, Princeton Review Online

Guide to Grammar and Style—by Jack Lynch, http://andromeda.rutgers
.edu/~jlynch/Writing. "Excellent reference guide for all writers for those
times when you can't decide between a comma and a semicolon. Also
includes usage tips."

Hotbot, http://www.hotbot.com. "If it's not there, it doesn't exist."—Joey
Anuff (see interview, page 47), Suck (see listing, page 172)

Inkspot, http://www.inkspot.com. "Inkspot has market info, articles, a great
e-newsletter, and excellent advice from successful writers on breaking in
and staying there. It also has lots of links to other equally worthy sites."
—Ellen Ullman

Kvetch, http://www.kvetch.com.—Noah Robischon's time waster, Netley News

Literary Arts Webring, The, http://www.lit-arts.com/WebRing/RingIndex .html.—Ellen Ullman, Princeton Review Online

Media Central, http://www.mediacentral.com. "Competent one-stop source for daily media news."—Joey Anuff, Suck

Misc.Writing Web Site, http://www.scalar.com/mw. "Useful articles and resources as well as providing a fascinating glimpse into the misc.writing community."

Mississippi Review, The, http://sushi.st.usm.edu/mrw. "During my precious moments of time-wasting, I look at literary magazines. They're my secret shame."—Alice Bradley, Charged

Missouri Review, The, http://www.missouri.edu/~moreview/main.html. "Another literary magazine I consult during my precious moments of time-wasting."—Alice Bradley, Charged

Poets & Writers Online, http://www.pw.org. "A plethora of info, ranging from networking opportunities to directories to classifieds. If there's a conference or workshop happening, you'll find out about it here.—Ellen Ullman, Princeton Review Online

Random Quotations, http://www.starlingtech.com/quotes/randquote.cgi. "I dare you to hit reload only once."—Debbie Ridpath Ohi's (see interview, page 39) time-waster site

Reporter's Guide to Internet Mailing Lists, The, http://www.daily.umn.edu/ ~broeker/guide.html.—Noah Robischon, Netley News

Salon, http://www.salon1999.com. "Still one of the best-written and designed zines on the Web. The articles are thought-provoking, original, and insightful. It's the best place for book reviews and to read about what makes other writers tick."—Ellen Ullman, Princeton Review Online. "One of the three best sites in terms of content. I just like reading it—which I guess is the best anyone can say about a Web magazine."—Alice Bradley, Charged

Slate, http://www.slate.com. "Don't believe the anti-hype. Surprisingly, amongst the Web's finest."—Joey Anuff, Suck

Stating the Obvious, http://www.theobvious.com.—Noah Robischon, Netley News

Suck, http://www.suck.com. "Another flavor of writing indigenous to the Web, and they wrote a hilarious guide for Web writers that's a must-read."—Marisa Bowe, Word

Walter Miller, http://www.geocities.com/Heartland/Prairie/9179/walter .htm. "One of the true virtuosos of the Web, Walter Miller is best described as a lobotomized, crack-smoking William Faulkner."—Marisa Bowe, Word

Web of Online Dictionaries, http://www.facstaff.bucknell.edu/rbeard/ diction.html. "Just enter your word and hit Return to search Merriam-Webster's Collegiate Dictionary, or search other types of dictionaries." —Debbie Ridpath Ohi, Inkspot (see listing, page 136)

Word, http://www.word.com. "One of the three best sites in terms of content. Word also does the most with their design."—Alice Bradley, Charged

Yahoo, http://www.yahoo.com. "Your first stop for research—better than its reputation suggests."—Joey Anuff, Suck

APPENDIX 2

Web Writing Resources Recommended by Online Writers

About.com, http://about.com/. "Sections for all sorts of other occupations. Sometimes I use it to get a snapshot of what another profession is like." —Angela Eaton (see interview, page 64)

About.com, Freelance Writers, http://freelancewrite.about.com. This site combines an extensive collection of useful Net links with feature articles that offer guidance, advice, and specific instruction for various freelance writing challenges (and I'm the guide!).—Kimberly Hill. "They also have jobs posted on a bulletin board, and have lots of good links."—June Campbell (see interview on page 66)

Allmusic Guide, http://www.allmusic.com. "Simply the ultimate resource for information on any artist's discography, a band's personnel, or which records a particular song was on. Though their picks for best record are often flawed, the info itself is usually right, easy to get to, and clearly presented."—Mike McGonigal (see interview on page 53)

America Online, Member Directory. "A keyword screen pops up and you enter 'editor' or 'producer' or 'publisher' and if someone has listed a member profile and those words are in it, you're in touch. I met the editor of my Writer's Guide book that way and got a deal two weeks later."—Skip Press (see interview, page 57)

ASJA Web Page, http://www.asja.org. "The American Society of Journalists and Authors is the nation's leading organization of independent nonfiction writers."—Daphne Clair (see interview, page 51)

Avalanche of Jobs for Writers, http://people.delphi.com/eide491/jobs .html. "They have lots of job listings. I have found work a couple of times from this site."—June Campbell

CNET, http://www.cnet.com.—Gary Welz (see interview, page 44)

Canada Newswire, http://www.newswire.ca. "Admittedly parochial, but their archives are searchable, and you can file your press releases about book releases, sales, etc., online. Handy."—Tracy Cooper-Posey (see interview, page 64)

Contentious, http://www.contentious.com. This is Amy Gahran's e-zine specifically for online writers. While the world is full of programmers and Web designers with advice about online content, this is one of the few publications targeted just to us.—Kimberly Hill

Copyright Basics, ftp://ftp.loc.gov/pub/copyright/circs/circ01.html#rp. "Know your rights when it comes to contracts and how there is negotiating room with almost all contracts."—Christina Tourigny (see interview, page 41)

Copyright Web Site, http://www.benedict.com. "Again, know your rights." —Christina Tourigny

Dejanews, http://www.dejanews.com. "Search engine that searches newsgroups. Useful for industry gossip, such as looking for other writers' comments and opinions on publishers and agents."—Tracy Cooper-Posey

Discovery Channel Online, http://www.discover.com. "For fun and good reading, I think the Discovery Channel Online is putting out some of the best online journalism to be found anywhere; it provides a good model for what's current in the field. And the subject matter is always interesting." —Michael Ray Taylor (see interview, page 59)

Email Media, http://www.ping.at/gugerell/media/index.htm. "The man that maintains this Web page (Peter Gugerell) has more markets on this site than any other site I have ever been to. He has markets in the U.S., Australia, Austria, Canada, and several miscellaneous countries as well. Again, this is one of the first places I went to and broke into online markets as well as several print markets. With this one site a writer could very easily spend a few weeks sending out queries. This is a great way for a 'starving' writer to get information, guidelines, and e-mail info without having to spend anything on postage. Peter is also a very nice man. He asks you to let him know if any of the markets are out of date, or if any new markets should be added, etc."—Christina Tourigny

Excite, http://www.excite.com.—Gary Welz

Feed, http://www.feed.com. The Feed daily columns are consistently well thought out and engaging. Feed really points to the limitless potential for good writing on the Web—it's like Salon if it were manageable and lived up to the hype.—Mike McGonigal

Google.com, http://www.google.com. This is a search engine that tends to yield really good results no matter what you're looking for.—Mike McGonigal

Grammar Lady, The, http://www.grammarlady.com. "All the embarrassing editing questions that you are supposed to already know the answers to. Love this woman. She has an 800 number too."—Angela Eaton

Hollywood Network, The, http://www.hollywoodnetwork.com. "Paying members can search for writing ads in the Hollywood Network's Acquisition Needs section."—Skip Press

Hollywood Reporter, The, http://www.hollywoodreporter.com. "The HR also lets you search their [writing] ads if you're a paying member."—Skip Press

ICQ, http://www.icq.com. "My timewaster site/service. It has chat and e-mail capabilities, bulletin boards and home pages."—Deborah Clark (see interview, page 52)

Inkspot Magazine, http://www.inkspot.com.—Geri Anderson (see interview, page 49). "Useful list of online writing tips."—Paul Vee (see interview, page 55). "Great site for writers, free newsletter and lots of info." —Daphne Clair. "A great starting point especially for beginning writers."—Deborah Clark. "Good all-around information, market links." —June Campbell. "One of the premier general information sites for writers. The free biweekly newsletter (subscribe@inkspot.com) makes it worthwhile, and I've yet to find any completely useless links. This is one of my most constantly visited sites."—Tracy Cooper-Posey

Internet Movie Database, The, http://www.imdb.com. "It's the best resource going (that you don't have to pay for) to look up producer, director, production company credits."—Skip Press

Internet World On-line, http://www.internetworld.com. "Very professional online journalism. Also a good online paying market."—Tracy Cooper-Posey

Internet Writer's Guideline Listing, The, http://wane5.scri.fsu.edu/~jtillman/DEV/ZDMS. "It offers guidelines to several online publications. Very helpful resource."—Christina Tourigny

John Labovitz's E-Zine Lists, http://www.meer.net/~johnl/e-zine-list/. "Has about 2500+ markets there, though you usually have to query to find out who pays. John likes to hear from the writers. He likes feedback. Good site and very helpful, especially to new writers."—Christina Tourigny

L-Soft, http://www.lsoft.com/lists/listref.html. "I really recommend the listservs to writers so they can find writing groups that they can share their info with and get new info from as well. You'd be surprised at what the right writers' group can do for your career as a writer, and how much you can help others as you become a 'veteran.' "—Christina Tourigny

Los Angeles County Coroner's Gift Shop Page, The, http://www.lacoroner.com/coroner.html. "One of those bizarre, inexplicable phenoms that are found only in cyberspace."—Patrick J. Kiger (see interview, page 61) on his time waster

Macintouch, http://www.macintouch.com. "The original Mac news and information site. Ditzing with one's computer, keeping up on the latest software, etc., is the greatest trap/time-wasting/procrastinatory thing there is because it almost feels like you're doing something—I mean, you're at the computer, after all."—Paul Vee

Microzoo.com, http://www.microzoo.com/links.html. "The best list I've found of newspapers across the nation."—Patrick J. Kiger

Mind's Eye Fiction, http://thetale.com. "They are very professional in their dealings and have an impressive collection of work—including stories from Stephen King, David Brin, Harlan Ellison. Five of their authors have received preliminary nominations in the Nebula Awards.—Tracy Cooper-Posey

National Writers Union, http://www.nwu.org/nwu/index.htm. "Their home page is one of the most valuable resources I have come across. There are very few writers I know that don't have this site bookmarked. It offers job resources, writer organizations, media and news, magazine rates, copyright information, dictionary and references, and links to a wide range of resources."—Christina Tourigny. "The 'members only' section has info about people's experiences with various markets—pay rates, openness to negotiation, how they work with you editorially—which is useful (mostly print, as I recall, but that may have changed now). There's also background info about all sorts of business issues freelancers face—contracts, rights, etc."—Bruce Mirken (see interview, page 42)

Newsgroups: Misc.writing and Alt.writing. "Misc.writing is especially entertaining and occasionally I get a gem from the rank and file. Most of the writers in that group are pretty responsive and responsible. I actually have about a half a dozen newsgroups that I prowl, but I'm hesitant to get involved too much because many of the discussions seem odd."—Jan Grieco

Nme.Com, http://www.nme.com. "For stupid gossip on limey music, this is where to go."—Mike McGonigal

New York Times on the Web, http://www.nytimes.com. "Because it's the Times. Plus, the paper of record's coverage of the early days of downloadable music—particularly that by Neil Strauss—has proven invaluable to anyone interested in the future of music."—Mike McGonigal

Perfect Sound Forever, http://www.furious.com/perfect. "Among the best fan sites ever assembled, this one takes on important musicians and genres in total depth with the sort of total love one used to only find in the best fanzines. The writing is clean and the interviews always illuminating."—Mike McGonigal

PR Newswire, http://www.prnewswire.com.—Gary Welz

Publishers Weekly, http://www.bookwire.com/pw/pw.html. "The [book] industry [periodical] online. Good for keeping in touch."—Tracy Cooper-Posey

Resource Page for Editors, A, http://www.talewins.com/. "Keep an eye on it."—Jan Grieco

Silicon Investor, http://www.techstocks.com. "My current obsession/vice." —Gary Welz

Staffwriters.com, http://www.staffwriters.com. "For tips and updates on online writing, I like the newsletter maintained by Staffwriters.com, and online writer referral service. (I make no claim for the service, but I like their newsletter.)"—Michael Ray Taylor

Tripod, http://www.tripod.com.—Jan Grieco

Vanessa Grant's Home Page, http://www.vgrant.com. "Software, books, tapes for writers, and links to writer and publisher sites."—Daphne Clair

Word, http://www.word.com "For innovative design and stunning writing that tends toward the hilarious and the extreme, you can't beat Word, one of the first professional (paying) literary Web sites."—Mike McGonigal

Writer's Guidelines Database, The, http://mav.net/guidelines—Todd Pitock (see interview, page 37); "Mostly print guidelines but some are for mags that I haven't run across in my many searches. Gives you ideas."—Angela Eaton

Writer's Page Newsletter, The, http://www.getset.com/writers.—Jan Grieco

Writer's Resource Center, http://www.azstarnet.com/~poewar/writer/writer.html.—Jan Grieco

Writerswrite, http://www.writerswrite.com. "Another good site—markets, interviews, newsletter, etc."—Daphne Clair; "A source for potential markets."—Skip Press

WWWebster Dictionary, http://www.w.m-w.com/dictionary.htm. "Includes a thesaurus."—Angela Eaton

APPENDIX 3

Online Market Questionnaire

Submission Guidelines

1. Publication title, subtitle, and URL:
2. Name of publishing company:
3. Mailing address:
   Tel.:   Fax:
   E-mail address for editorial submissions:
   (e-mail address must be included)
4. Name and title of top editor:
5. What percentage of your publication is freelance written?
6. Brief editorial description of your publication and its audience:
7. Established (month, year):
8. Circulation in unique visits—not "hits"—per month:
   (We'd rather print even an unverified estimate than "circulation withheld.")
9. (Please check box with "x") Pays on [ ] Acceptance [ ] Publication
   [ ] Other__ (explain)
10. Byline given? [ ] Yes [ ] No [ ] Sometimes
11. What rights do you purchase?
12. Do you accept submissions that are [ ] simultaneous [ ] previously published [ ] electronic
13. Reports in [_____ how long] on queries? [_____ How long] on manuscripts?
14. Editorial Needs: In the following list of article subjects, please put an "x" in those you use and add any not listed.
    [ ] book excerpts [ ] entertainment [ ] erotica [ ] essays
    [ ] exposé [ ] health/fitness [ ] how-to [ ] humor
    [ ] fiction [ ] general interest [ ] historical [ ] inspirational

[ ] interview [ ] men's [ ] music [ ] new product
[ ] opinion [ ] personal experience [ ] poetry [ ] religious
[ ] technical [ ] technology [ ] teen [ ] trade
[ ] travel [ ] sports [ ] women's [ ] other__ (explain)

15. Should the writer [ ] Query [ ] Query with published clips [ ] Send complete manuscript.
16. Word length for articles? Minimum_____ Maximum_____
17. Payment for assigned articles: Minimum_____ Maximum_____ (If "varies," please add usual range.)
    Payment for unsolicited articles? Minimum_____ Maximum_____
18. Does your publication pay the expenses of writers on assignment?
    [ ] Yes [ ] No [ ] Sometimes

Photos/Art

19. Freelancers should [ ] State availability of photos with submission [ ] Send photos with submission
20. Payment policy on photos? [ ] min._____ max._____ [ ] no additional
    [ ] negotiates individually
21. Requirements? [ ] Captions [ ] Model releases [ ] Identification of subjects
22. Rights purchased on photos? [ ] one-time [ ] all [ ] other_____

Advice

23. Please cite an Internet address for additional online guidelines, if available, but also please use this space to briefly explain how freelancers can query and write for you more effectively. Be as specific with your tips as possible. Any common/frustrating mistakes made by freelancers? Any specific kinds of articles you don't want to see?

Subject Index

General Interest

(Including Animals, Art, Astrology/New Age, Beauty, Cigars, Contemporary Culture, Cooking, Education, Entertainment, Erotica, Food, Gardening, Health/ Fitness, Home, Humor, Leisure, Love/Sex/Relationships, Movies, Nature, News, Nutrition, Wine) (See also "Regional Guides")

Lifestyle

(Including Disabilities, Gay/Lesbian Interest, Men's, Outdoors, Parenting, Teen/Young Adult, Religion, Women's) (See also "Regional Guides")

Literary

(Including Fiction, Mystery, Poetry, Romance, Science Fiction, Fantasy)

Regional Guides

(Including Local Entertainment, Food, Gay/Lesbian Interests, Music, Opinion, Sports, Travel)

Sports

(Including Baseball, Basketball, Fishing, Football, Golf, Guns, Motor Sports, Soccer, Surfing, Tennis)

Technology

Trade

(Including Advertising, Books, Business, Career, E-Commerce, Education, Electronic Book Publishers, Fashion, Finance, Journalism/Writing, Marketing)

Travel

(See also "Regional Guides")

5/00 - 9/03 9